T0318923

NOTICE TO READERS

Compensation as a Strategic Asset: The New Paradigm does not represent an official position of the American Institute of Certified Public Accountants, and it is distributed with the understanding that the author and the publisher are not rendering legal, accounting, or other professional services in the publication. If legal advice or other expert assistance is required, the services of a competent professional should be sought.

COMPENSATION AS A STRATEGIC ASSET

The New Paradigm

August J. Aquila, Ph.D.
Coral L. Rice

Issued in association with the
PCPS Management of an
Accounting Practice Committee

1001-344

ISBN 978-0-87051-659-7

DEDICATION

To Emily, my companion through life's ups and downs, and to Merle Simmons, Ph.D., a lifelong friend, mentor, and teacher.

August J. Aquila

To my parents, Keith and Pat, who believed in me and who still push me, gently and not-so-gently when I need it. To Kyle, who appreciated his working mom and grew into one of the finest gentlemen I've ever known. And finally, to Dave, the rock that holds down the fort and supports me no matter what.

Coral L. Rice

ABOUT THE AUTHORS

August J. Aquila, Ph.D.

 August J. Aquila, an internationally known consultant, speaker and author, has held leading positions in the accounting profession for more than a quarter of a century. He currently heads AQUILA Global Advisors, a full-service consulting firm to accounting and other professional services firms. August focuses his practice on resolving management and owner issues, helping firms develop and implement strategic plans and facilitating firm retreats. August is also one of the top consultants in the area of mergers & acquisitions, having been involved in more than 100 transactions.

Before starting AQUILA Global Advisors, August held several executive leadership positions with American Express Tax and Business Services. He also was a partner in a top-50 firm. In 2003 he was elected into the Association for Accounting Marketing's Hall of Fame and in 2004 he was selected as one of the Top 100 Most Influential People in the Accounting Profession.

August is the author of hundreds of articles and several books on practice management, mergers & acquisitions, and marketing. He is the co-author, most recently, of *Client at the Core: Marketing and Managing Today's Professional Services Firm* (John Wiley & Sons).

August lives in Minnetonka, Minnesota, with his wife, Emily, and their poodle, Skyler. For more information about August, visit www.Aquila Advisors.com or contact him at aaquila@aquilaadvisors.com.

Coral L. Rice

Coral L. Rice is one of the top consultants in the areas of organizational development, human resources, and learning services. She has helped many firms clarify mission, vision, values, and strategic direction.

She possesses unique expertise in diagnosing and designing firms' people systems and processes (for example, recruitment, retention, and succession) to support strategic goals. She has provided direction to accounting firms in the redesign of their performance management and compensation systems for both partners and staff so they reward character and competence and pay for performance.

One of Coral's strengths is her ability to teach, coach, and guide clients in accomplishing their personal and professional goals. She developed The Growth Partnership's renowned workshop, *The Reluctant Salesperson: A Realistic Approach to Practice Development for the CPA*™ as well as its partner development program, The Partner Institute™. She also facilitates group workshops and coaches partners in a variety of subjects, including business development and leadership.

Before joining The Growth Partnership, Coral served the FranklinCovey Company for many years in a variety of consulting, sales, and sales leadership roles. She was also responsible for creating Franklin Covey's Knowledge EpiCenter®, the firm's knowledge management system.

Coral and her husband, Dave, enjoy golf, volunteering, and sharing time with their son, Kyle, and other family members and friends.

CONTENTS

FOREWORD

by
Richard Caturano, CPA
Managing Partner Vitale, Caturano & Co. PC

The myriad challenges faced by today's professional service firm leaders are daunting. For as long as I can remember, the number one challenge facing us has been staffing and the shortage of talent. As times change, this issue will not go away. Rather, it will get more complex. The shortage of Ph.D.s to train the next generation of professionals is alarming. Competition for talent from all areas of the United States and abroad.

Work/life balance is at the forefront of the minds of the most recent generations of professionals. The lack of diversity in our firms is becoming even more acute. Compensating our partners and staff in a manner that not only leads them to do the right things, but also rewards them for helping the firm achieve its strategic initiatives now ranks as one of the key issues facing accounting firms.

What then is a leader of a professional service firm to do? While we have learned much about having the right mission, the right vision, the right values, the right strategy, the right people (in the right places, of course), we still struggle with how to bring all these factors in alignment. In my view the key success factor is how all of these elements relate to and work off of each other to create a successful firm. In *Compensation as a Strategic Asset*, August Aquila and Coral Rice, two veteran consultants to the accounting profession, develop the essential blueprint for helping firms with a holistic approach for creating an effective compensation method.

Interdependence, alignment, synergy, win-win, rewards for performance—these sound like old-fashioned buzz words and concepts, often over-used and misunderstood in today's business world. That may be so, but in this rapidly changing business environment, they remain important elements of the successful firm. The authors take us step-by-step through a process that brings mission, vision, values, strategy, leadership, goal-setting, performance management and compensation together.

I know personally that when the various components of our strategy work off each other, the investment in the numerous costly initiatives which are required to compete is easier to justify. When our actions align with our strategy, we get countless positive benefits, including those which enable us to attract, motivate and retain the talent so desperately needed in our firms. When the sum of our actions is greater than the whole, success, regardless of how each firm defines it, usually follows.

Compensation as a Strategic Asset breaks theory down to practical steps in a way that is understandable, and more importantly, actionable. Aquila's and Rice's hands-on experience and pragmatic approach are explained in a context which not only makes sense, but can be applied to firms of any size. They provide a process that allows each firm to develop its own mission, vision, unique values and compensation system.

This is an extremely well-written book and should be required reading for every managing partner. If you follow their advice, you will develop a compensation model that drives a well-defined mission, vision, and strategy. Your compensation system, too, will become a strategic asset.

Richard Caturano, CPA
Vitale Caturano & Company (Boston, MA).

Mr. Caturano is a past chair of the
Private Companies Practice Section of AICPA.

PREFACE

While there are many topics that generate a wide range of feelings and emotions in accounting firms, the topic of how to compensate firm owners is certainly one that generates some of the widest and most volatile emotions. So, why would anyone want to tackle a book about owner and staff compensation plans? It would seem to be a fool's errand.

It has often been said a lack of money is the root of all evil. Maybe that explains, in part, why there is so much disagreement among CPA firm owners. We believe this book can help CPA firm owners and other professional services firm owners learn not only how to split the compensation pie, but significantly grow the pie by aligning compensation plans to the firm's mission, vision, values and strategy.

Many firms struggle with compensation issues not merely because of the allocation of income, but also because of the overall economic performance of the firm.

This book then is as much about growing the pie as it is about using compensation as a strategic asset to split the pie in an effort to recruit, reward, and retain more effectively.

The best way to root out the so-called "evil" is to increase the amount of money the firm can allocate. While having *more* money to distribute may keep disagreements at a minimum, money alone does not necessarily mean the compensation system rewards the right things and allows for fair distribution. As we will demonstrate, money only solves part of the problem.

Compensation systems, programs, and methods by themselves do not generate sustained positive results for a firm. In the nineteenth century, the French novelist, Gustave Flaubert wrote; "Success is a consequence, not a goal." Success doesn't happen because we wish ourselves to be successful. Firms are not successful because partners simply want them to be. Successful firms develop and implement processes that fundamentally change and nurture the relationship between owners and employees and the firms for which they both work.

The other piece of the compensation dilemma, allocation, also needs to be addressed. Unless a firm has a fair compensation system that is easy to understand, no amount of money can root out all the "evil." Compensation policies and practices must also align with other elements of a firm, especially the firm's culture and values. Finally, a credible compensation system supports and is tied to the firm's mission, vision, and strategy.

Successful firms don't just happen. They have good leaders and good employees who strive each day to achieve mission and vision by living the firms' values and carrying out strategy. In other words, they *work* at being successful. They execute! And they reward for performance rather than entitlement.

Compensation may not be the only reason we work, but it is often a necessity in our lives. The amount of money we earn is often perceived as a measure of our personal and professional value. At the same time, most of us recognize that it is not only about money. We also want a positive work environment, a sense of personal and professional growth, and an opportunity to contribute to something larger than ourselves.

Poorly designed compensation systems and their lack of perceived fairness can fracture firms, encourage owners to look elsewhere, create feelings of despair and angst, and cause frustration and dissension among owners and employees. In turn, most owners realize they can achieve more by working together than by working in silos, but they're unsure about how to create a compensation system that rewards for both independent and interdependent accomplishment.

Firms are comprised of human beings, and a good compensation system should reflect its stakeholders' needs. And while there may never be enough money to satisfy everyone completely, there should be sound ways that help firm leaders make good decisions about who should be paid what and explain to partners and employees why they earn what they earn. Thomas Jefferson may have captured the current compensation situation best when he wrote, "There is nothing more unequal than the equal treatment of unequal people."

Jay R. Schuster and Patricia K. Zingheim write, "Most (research) suggests that organizations that are able to design their pay programs to pay the best performers better than other performers are able to accomplish several important organizational imperatives:

- Making excellent performance financially worthwhile.
- Communicating to satisfactory performers the importance of acceptable and better performance.
- Communicating to less than satisfactory performers that their performance must improve or they will be encouraged to find employment where their abilities more closely match the performance expectations of the organization."[1]

[1]Jay R. Schuster and Patricia K. Zingheim, *The New Pay: Linking Employee and Organizational Performance* (San Francisco: Jossey-Bass, 1996), pp. 19-20.

This book is written for firm leaders and owners who are interested in learning how to do so—how to align compensation to the firm's mission, vision, values, and goals. We also examine the key characteristics of the most common current compensation systems and provide results from the first comprehensive compensation survey among CPA firms conducted by us and the PCPS Division of the AICPA.

What we share in this book is a new perspective on the crucial subject of designing an effective compensation system based on the needs of your firm. We know from experience that each compensation system can succeed, and each can also fail. There is no perfect compensation system. The real challenge is to design a compensation system that aligns financial rewards with the firm's strategic direction.

We hold that compensation and performance should be linked. And performance evaluation should take into account both the financial (objective measures) and nonfinancial (subjective measures) aspects of creating value in the firm. It should also take into account and measure both leading and lagging measures of success.

Compensation as a Strategic Asset also lays out a framework and methodology that will not only help a firm get top notch results, but also provides a step-by-step process on how to create an effective compensation program. First, stakeholder (such as owner, employee, or client) needs must be identified. Second, each firm needs to develop its unique mission, vision, values and a strategy—all of which are designed to meet stakeholder needs. Third, authentic and effective leaders must drive appropriate goal-setting and performance management systems to accomplish the above. These systems should focus on overall profitability and a variety of factors beyond the traditional measurements of chargeable time, revenue growth and origination.

Owners and employees who help the firm execute its strategies should share most in its profits. We provide workable solutions for profit allocation. While many of the techniques we describe are not new, we share how to apply them in new and different ways.

The goal of this book is to share with you our experiences, insights and views on this critical aspect of firm management. We hope it adds to the existing body of knowledge and stirs additional dialogue about CPA firm compensation plans.

August J. Aquila
Minnetonka, MN

Coral Rice
St. Louis, MO
April 1, 2007

ACKNOWLEDGMENTS

No book is written solely by its authors. When many practitioners and consultants add to the body of knowledge about compensation systems on a regular basis, a book couldn't, nor shouldn't, be written solely by its authors.

The writings of Dr. Stephen R. Covey have had a profound influence on our thinking about principle-centered leadership and the concepts of both win-win thinking and win-win systems, especially compensation systems. We also acknowledge Stephen M.R. Covey, Keith Gulledge, and many others from the FranklinCovey Company.

Consultants learn by helping clients become successful, and in that process, we often find we learn as much, if not more, than we teach our clients. So, to all of the clients with which we have worked over many years, we say, "Thank You!" A special thanks to Bruce Malott and Tom Burrage at Meyners + Company who were up for a challenge and allowed Coral to learn a lot about what to do and what not to do to help firms design better compensation systems.

We could not have written this book without the help of many people: accounting practitioners, members of the legal profession, fellow consultants, and our spouses and children. Each contributed something that challenged or enlarged our thinking—sometimes even causing us to change our points of view. Their comments, suggestions, and critiques have improved the final product.

The list of contributors is long, and those not listed here are not for lack of appreciation, but for lack of time and space. Among those who have influenced us over the years are, Patrick McKenna, Edge International, one of the most creative consultants to professional services firms and Bruce Marcus, a long-time friend and mentor to August as well as an early pioneer in the field of professional services firm marketing and the author of The Marcus Letter (www.marcusletter.com).

Thanks to Jane S. Roesti, the Director of Excellence for the Missouri Department of Conservation, who taught Coral many things about adult learning, but more importantly, about life. And not enough can be said about Howard Rosen at Conner Ash P.C. who is a trusted client, colleague, and friend.

Thanks to Richard Rinehart for sharing with us his views on absolute and relative compensation; to Marc Rosenberg, a longtime colleague whose annual Rosenberg Survey contributes valuable statistical information to the accounting profession; and to Chris Frederiksen, who is always openly willing to share his knowledge. We also want to thank Richard Caturano, managing partner of Vitale, Caturano & Company and Bill Herman, Managing Partner of Plante & Moran, PLLC for sharing their thoughts on partner compensation with us.

We wish to thank Altman Weil, Inc., for sharing with us their compensation survey of the legal profession as well as James Cotterman, a principal at Altman Weil, Inc. and leading compensation consultant to the legal profession, whose writings and thoughts are scattered throughout this book.

We thank the following individuals for their contributions by allowing us to work with them and their firms and sharing their knowledge and tools:

- Michael Epstein, Managing Partner of Fuller Landau and Partner-in-charge of Corporate Finance Advisory Services
- Ray Roberts, Managing Partner of Accounting & Consulting Group, LLP
- Howard Rosen, Principal and President of Conner Ash P.C.

We are grateful to Monica Tapp, Human Resources and Organizational Development Consultant at The Growth Partnership, who provided significant contribution in the compensation survey design and compilation. Without her assistance and analysis, we still would be going through more than 400 responses. Thanks also go to Jeffrey S. Pawlow, Charles Hylan, and Lisa Benson at The Growth Partnership.

A vast measure of gratitude goes to our editor, Laura Inge, for her help in managing this project, the members of the PCPS Executive Committee Task Force who provided direction for and reviews of this book and to Jim Metzler, American Institute of Certified Public Accountants, Vice-President, Small Firm Division and the PCPS Division, for sponsoring the 2006 Compensation Survey.

Readers of *Client at the Core: Marketing and Managing Today's Professional Services Firm* (Wiley 2004) by August Aquila and Bruce W. Marcus will recognize a number of ideas in this book, especially those in Chapters 5 and 10.

Finally, we want to thank our spouses for putting up with two busy consultants who still found time to write this book and keep their marriages intact.

August J. Aquila and Coral L. Rice

April 1, 2007

The following are members of the Private Companies Practice Section Executive Committee Task Force who provided direction for and reviews of this book.

Richard J. Caturano, CPA
Vitale, Caturano & Co. PC
Boston, Massachusetts

Frederick R. Kostecki, CPA
RubinBrown, LLP
Saint Louis, Missouri

Ronald Thompkins, CPA
Watson Rice, LLP
Miami, Florida

AICPA Staff:

Acquisitions	Laura Inge
Editors	Karen M. Coutinho, Margot Faivush, and Michelle Partridge-Doerr
Production	Lainie Burke Rosenthal

1

WHY WE NEED A NEW COMPENSATION PARADIGM

"All significant breakthroughs are significant break-'withs' old ways of thinking."

—Thomas Kuhn

If you are reading this book, you are likely only somewhat satisfied or even dissatisfied with your firm's current owner compensation system and you are wondering how to make it better. Or perhaps you want to benchmark your current compensation system against firms that are known for their best practices. Whatever your reasons for reading this book, you can make your current compensation system more effective, and perhaps even fairer, than it is today.

While the world in which the professional works today is vastly different from the traditional environment during the first 90 years of the twentieth century, compensation systems have not changed much during the same period. Practicing in the twenty-first century poses significant challenges to accounting firm owners in the areas of leadership, management, risk vs. reward, recruitment and retention, succession, and compensation.

This chapter discusses paradigm shifts in the accounting profession and paradigm shifts in owner compensation.

PARADIGM SHIFTS IN THE ACCOUNTING PROFESSION

No one can predict the future with accuracy, but we know what has worked in the past often no longer suffices in the new world order of the twenty-first century. We base this statement on our observations of the public accounting profession for more than 25 years, and we recognize the following realities:

- Global outsourcing
- Competitive landscape
- Increased regulation
- Advancements in technology
- Global economy

- Fee pressure
- Client demands
- Firm leadership
- New metrics
- Compensation
- Workplace diversity
- Work-life balance
- Generational differences
- Talent shortage

A discussion of each paradigm shift in the profession follows.

Global Outsourcing

The professional services sectors (law, accounting, and medicine) in the United States are beginning to feel pressures of the global economy. Accounting and tax preparation work is now outsourced to India or other countries, legal research is often contracted, and various activities such as medical practices are performed in locations far removed from the patient.

Competitive Landscape

In the first few years of the twenty-first century, the accounting profession faced some of its darkest hours. It is no exaggeration to state that the profession was shaken to its core. Arthur Andersen, one of the premier international accounting firms, was not only disgraced but destroyed. Never in the history of the accounting profession had one of the big international accounting firms gone out of business in this fashion. The catastrophic events of an Enron, WorldCom, or Adelphia; advances in technology; and increased client sophistication have contributed to the current environment in which accountants must now work and compete.

Increased Regulation

Public company auditors are now regulated by the Public Company Accounting Oversight Board (PCAOB) an agency created under the Sarbanes-Oxley Act (SOX), the 2002 corporate governance reform act. SOX was passed not only to oversee the auditors of public companies, but also to protect the interests of investors and further public interest in the preparation of informative, fair, and independent audit reports.

Advancements in Technology

Technology, such as the use of Web-based accounting and payroll solutions, plays an increasingly important role in today's public accounting practice, regardless of the size of the firm. Technology allows any firm to have tax returns, write-up, and other backroom procedures processed in India, another low-cost country, or even a low-cost area in the United States. In his groundbreaking book, *The World Is Flat: A Brief History of the Twenty-First Century*, Thomas L. Friedman shares, "In 2003, some

25,000 U.S. tax returns were done in India. In 2004 the number was 100,000. In 2005, it is expected to be 400,000. In a decade, you will assume that your accountant has outsourced the basic preparation of your tax returns—if not more."[1]

Global Economy

The United States and other developed countries of the world are feeling the impact of a global economy. Many industries (such as automotive, manufacturing, and textile) have undergone, or are undergoing, widespread economic restructuring. Accounting firms of all sizes are beginning to feel some of the same global pressures. Like other businesses, they have no choice—they either generate a profit or they go out of business.

Fee Pressure

Fee pressure on basic or commodity services, such as bookkeeping or simple tax compliance, will increase over the next decade. Firms that are unable to maintain acceptable profit margins on commodity work, especially when commodity work comprises a large percentage of their practices, may have insufficient cash to allocate to owners. This will only cause more owner dissention and place additional pressure on owners to create compensation systems that reward for performance rather than entitlement.

Client Demands

We recently conducted a survey of more than 100 accounting firms for the Association of Accounting Firm Administrators. The survey showed that clients of the very smallest to the very largest firms are more sophisticated today than ever before. Clients continue to become more sophisticated in basic tax and financial issues. They have access to an overwhelming abundance of data and online resources that deal with business operations, taxes, and finance. As a result, the days of the generalist are, perhaps, short lived. While clients are willing to pay for value-added services, it may be harder to demonstrate the added value your firm can provide. The traditional business model of the professional adviser as the expert is not where future demand will lie. While this model has well served the service professions (such as legal, medical, and public accounting), today's clients no longer see themselves as humble individuals asking experts for their "worldly advice." Professionals today collaborate with their clients to create exact solutions to individual and organizational problems. This requires the professional to have deeper knowledge and greater skills than ever before. The future, we believe, will require accountants to have specialized knowledge in industries and specific practice areas as well as greater consulting skills.

---

[1]Thomas L. Friedman, *The World Is Flat: A Brief History of the Twenty-First Century* (New York: Farrar, Straus and Giraux, 2003), p. 13.

Firm Leadership

Firms run the gamut from great leadership to poor leadership. Great leadership is often expressed in the achievement of the firm's goals and mission, and translates itself into higher productivity and profitability. While firm leadership has been shown as a major differentiating factor among certified public accounting firms, few firms invest in developing good, much less great, leaders. Worse yet, some professional services firm leaders may have outdated concepts about authentic leadership. According to Bruce J. Avolio and Fred Luthans in "The High Impact Leader," authentic leadership is a process that combines positive leader capacities and a highly developed organizational context.[2] The authentic leader is confident, hopeful, optimistic, resilient, moral/ethical, future-oriented, and gives priority to developing associates to be leaders. Authentic leaders are true to themselves and their behaviors positively transform or develop their associates into leaders themselves.

New Metrics

Forward-thinking leaders are embracing modern management techniques, such as the balanced scorecard, to manage and lead their firms. They realize that focusing on economic and financial indicators (measures) alone are insufficient to maintain a competitive edge and achieve desired levels of profitability and client service. They realize the need to focus on client service and loyalty, employee growth and learning, business development, and internal systems development indicators as well.

Compensation

Compensation and reward systems for employees and owners are being modified. At a time when many believe Generation Y maintains a strong sense of entitlement, there is also a growing trend in the corporate world to move from entitlement to performance-based compensation systems. Even older public accounting firms with entrenched beliefs are beginning to reward their top performers—those owners and employees who help the firm achieve its strategic vision. They are also beginning to let nonperformers and underperformers go. Employment for life, even for public accounting firm owners, is no longer guaranteed.

Workplace Diversity

The AICPA's Diversity Statement provides firms a clear vision of today's and tomorrow's workforce:

> The American Institute of Certified Public Accountants is committed to being recognized as the premier national professional organization. To achieve this status, it must lead in encouraging, valuing and fostering diversity in its membership and in the workforce. The AICPA has decided to reaffirm the

---

[2]Bruce J. Avolio and Fred Luthans, *The High Impact Leader* (New York: McGraw Hill, 2006).

importance of diversifying the accounting profession and promoting work-force diversity by making these objectives among the AICPA's highest priorities. Therefore, in principle and in practice, the AICPA will identify, recognize, and support strategies and efforts within the organization and profession that are dedicated to achieving the AICPA's diversity objectives.

The AICPA will begin by increasing its efforts to continue to recruit and maintain a diverse professional staff. In addition, it will continue to actively recruit and maintain diverse membership in all AICPA committees.

The AICPA encourages all state CPA societies and related organizations to adopt similar diversity statements.

Many firms are embracing the Institute's diversity statement. For example, in 2006 Ernst & Young LLP was honored as one of the "Top 50 Companies for Diversity" by *Diversity Inc* magazine. In recognition of the firm's commitment to workplace equity, Ernst & Young ranked 24 overall and ranked sixth on the magazine's "Top Ten Companies for GLBT [gay, lesbian, bisexual, and transgender] Employees" list. The firm also appeared for the eighth consecutive year on both the 2006 *Fortune* "100 Best Companies to Work For" list and *Working Mother's* "100 Best Companies for Working Mothers" list.

According to a recent study ("A Decade of Changes in the Accounting Profession: Workforce Trends and Human Capital Practices") conducted by the AICPA's Work-Life and Women's Initiatives Executive Committee, women now account for 19 percent of all public accounting firm owners. This is a 58 percent increase over the last 10 years. This trend will only increase based on the number of women graduating with degrees in accountancy. The report concluded that the accounting workforce is changing faster than human resources policies can adjust, noting significant gaps between what firms think motivates and retains people and what is effective in actual practice. (A copy of the report is available from the AICPA's Web site, www.aicpa.org/members/div/career/wofi/research.htm.)

Work-Life Balance

Market dynamics—single parents, children caring for aged parents, and children—are forcing firms to address the work-life balance. Both men and women in public accounting firms are taking advantage of alternative career paths now being offered by firms. These include flex time, part-time, and shared positions. A few firms are also offering part-time partnership positions to employees they want to keep.

The need for work-life balance, along with the overall shortage of qualified staff, has caused more firms to abandon their "up or out policy." According to the AICPA work-life study, 38 percent of firms surveyed offer some kind of alternative career path that does not lead to an owner position.

Generational Differences

According to Rick Telberg, Editor at Large at the AICPA, "It is well established that there are distinctly different personal preferences and work habits among the four generations in the workplace. For instance, as we reported in 'What Your Workforce Really Wants,' the generations fall in a few basic categories, the so-called Mature Generation, born before 1946; Baby Boomers, born between 1946 and 1964; Generation X, born between 1965 and 1980; and Generation Y, born after 1980."

According to Leslie Murphy, Former AICPA Chair, "In the next 15 years, 75 percent of current AICPA members will be reaching or approaching retirement age." The accounting profession's future will be controlled by the tail end of the Baby Boomers, those born after 1960, and Generation X. With four different generations currently in the ranks of all firms, it is inevitable that generational conflicts arise as the older generations try to hold onto what they have achieved and the newer generations strive to build for the future.

Talent Shortages

It was the best of times and it was the worst of times. If only Charles Dickens were writing today. Every firm in the country could use more people, especially experienced ones. Even though enrollment is up in accounting programs, it will be a few years before graduates enter the job market. Jerry Love, chairman elect of the Texas Society of Certified Public Accountants, captured the current environment when he said in a March 2006 article in the *Austin Business Journal*, "Right now we are just trading people. The shortage is not going to go away anytime in the near future. As the Baby Boomer generation begins to retire in increasing numbers in the coming years, firms will continue to strain to fill positions."

New paradigms are replacing old ones, and when there is a paradigm shift of this magnitude, massive change generally follows. The factors discussed in this chapter have caused firms to look differently at their resources and reward systems.

Joel Arthur Barker observed that "when a paradigm shifts, everyone goes back to zero."[3] By "zero," Barker meant that no matter what your position before the paradigm shift, you are back at the starting line. Everyone who is affected by the shift is starting over. No one has an advantage over anyone else. The old laws and rules no longer apply.

We maintain a paradigm shift is currently taking place in the area of firm compensation systems. Some firms will see it and embrace it, others will see it and laugh at it, and still others will not see it until it may be too late. Paradigm shifts generally do not happen overnight; they evolve as we receive new information or more complete information, and there is usually a transition period between the old and new paradigms. However, those firms that see the shift early and embrace it can gain competitive edge over those who laugh or do not see it until it is too late.

---

[3]Joel A. Baker, *Paradigms: The Business of Discovering the Future* (New York: Harper Business, 1993), p. 140.

Living through a paradigm shift, whether you see it or not, generally results in change—either small or large—and some pain. To give you an idea of what firms are going through today, we share the statement of a managing owner of one of our client firms after his firm made changes to its owner compensation system: "I will say this—change is chaotic, painful, unsettling, and hard." Need we say more?

PARADIGM SHIFTS IN OWNER COMPENSATION

Based on our consulting with firms and the 2006 compensation survey we conducted with the AICPA PCPS Division, we have identified 11 specific paradigm shifts taking place in public accounting firm owner compensation plans. These paradigm shifts are outlined in Exhibit 1–1, "Old Versus New Compensation Paradigms for Owners." A discussion of our observations follows.

Evaluating Based on Customized Criteria and Goals

In the old paradigm, firms often tended to evaluate all owners on the same criteria—business development, billable hours, and origination, to name a few—regardless of each owner's competence in these areas. Everyone was, in essence, put into the same mold.

Owners with valuable competencies outside of these criteria often were not motivated to exercise them since there was no reward for doing so. The old paradigm also paid little attention to managing the practice or to building future capacity in the firm. There were few, if any, incentives for an owner to cooperate with other owners, to develop future leaders, or to build new niches and services.

Owners focused on how they could achieve *their own* individual goals. Hence, firms created a culture of independence and competition: "I win and I do not care whether you win or lose," or worse, "I win, you lose." Success today is contingent upon the owners acting *interdependently* rather than independently.

The new paradigm takes into consideration the strategic and operational goals of the firm. It encourages the accomplishment of current production goals as well as goals that build the firm's ability to get even better results in the future—developing "capacity." These goals (for example, improving staff skills and creating more effective business systems) keep the firm capable of future growth. The ultimate, long-term success and viability of a firm depend upon the accomplishment of these two types of goals.

One chief operating officer (COO) of a Top 100 Accounting Firm compared his firm to a sports team: "The team has an overriding vision and mission and needs to fill various spots with people who have different but complementary competencies. The more members work together, the more successful the firm becomes."

Using Win-Win Agreements

Under the old paradigm, compensation was often allocated based on a pure formula calculation, some combination of formula and subjective evaluation or relative determination. The results of our 2006 Compensation Survey show that firms will be moving away from the formula compensation plan to the pay-for-performance approach.

The new paradigm requires each owner and the firm to determine mutually agreed upon expectations at the beginning of the year, and to identify what it means if the owner meets expectations. This is often called a "win-win agreement" because owners are generally focusing on goals that allow the owner to focus on his or her talents, passion, and activities (a win for them) that drive both short-term and long-term growth and profitability (a win for the firm). There is no confusion about what needs to be done by when or by whom.

Focusing on Current Production and Future Capacity

We often tell our clients that no margin means no mission. There certainly is nothing wrong with focusing on current production. After all, that is what helps to create profits today. That focus can become dysfunctional, however, when current production is the *only or primary* focus.

The new compensation paradigm suggests a firm needs to focus equally on current production as well as building capacity for future production, developing new services, creating future leaders, and training employees. Client needs are constantly changing and, in today's environment, clients will surely look to another firm if your firm cannot satisfy their needs.

Providing a Solid Safety Net

Under the old paradigm, many owners were left to swim or sink. Even if they were given goals at the beginning of the year, they were often left on their own to achieve them; they generally received no coaching, no mentoring, and no quarterly performance reviews. In short, firm management did not support its owners.

Under the new paradigm, for the firm to win, owners must be great swimmers. As a result, more resources may be provided to help owners achieve goals. This does not mean the firm will "carry" unproductive owners. Rather, it must provide them an environment in which they can succeed with the resources they need, and if they are unable to achieve their goals, they may be counseled graciously to find other opportunities.

Rewarding Performance

"What did you do for me today?" may be the new mantra. Seniority, equity, and business origination no longer count as much as they once did in the scheme of total compensation.

The worst case scenario under the old paradigm of entitlement is one in which owners are compensated solely based on seniority, equity, and even origination without regard to current production. For example, Owner Jones has 40 percent ownership. The firm's current compensation system provides for each owner to take out a draw of $100,000 and then profits are allocated based on ownership. Jones' other founding owner, Smith, has 38 percent ownership, and the four remaining owners have 7 percent, 6 percent, 5 percent, and 4 percent. Jones and Smith work the fewest hours and have the least billable time. Since a large portion of their compensation is based on ownership, they are able to remain the two highest-paid owners without contributing much to the firm today. Younger owners could rightfully argue that both Jones and Smith have effectively retired from the firm, but have failed to inform fellow owners.

The new paradigm shifts a greater percentage of total compensation from entitlement to performance. We see some firms limiting the percentage of total compensation based on seniority, equity and origination to as low as 10 percent. Several firms are between 10 percent and 20 percent.

Including At-Risk Compensation

A natural consequence of the current environmental and economic realities is that a lesser percentage of total compensation is being guaranteed to owners. In the old paradigm an owner could often draw 90 percent or more of his or her total compensation. For example, an owner making $250,000 per year would be guaranteed $225,000. The amount at risk ($25,000) would be insufficient to motivate the owner to perform at a high level or even worry about performance.

Under the new paradigm, that same owner might be guaranteed 60 percent or less of the total compensation or $150,000 ($250,000 × 60 percent). In fact, some of the most profitable firms pay owners 25 percent of their potential compensation during the year. The remainder is at risk.

In one firm with which we are familiar, the average owner total compensation was over $400,000 in 2003. Yet, owners were only allowed to draw $100,000 during the year. The rest was allocated as a performance bonus.

Ensuring Fairness

We cannot tell you how many owners have pulled us aside to talk about the perceived lack of fairness of their current compensation systems. While some of this complaining may be "sour grapes," there is proof that older systems were often not designed to be fair, and owners do indeed have a legitimate complaint. In our 2006 Compensation Survey, we asked, "To what extent is the owner compensation system designed to be fair to each owner in the firm?" Here are the responses:

1. Fifty-one percent believe their systems were designed to be very fair.
2. Forty-one percent believe their systems were designed to be somewhat fair.
3. Eight percent believe their systems were not designed to be fair at all.

We asked a follow-up question as to how fairly the compensation system is applied.

■ Sixty percent said very fairly.
■ Thirty-five percent indicted somewhat fairly.
■ Five percent reported not applied fairly at all.

A reliable compensation system not only needs to be understood by the owners, it also needs to be designed in a fair manner and then applied fairly. If owners do not understand how the compensation system works or, even worse, if they do not know what to do during the year to earn their compensation or increase it, a feeling of unfairness can permeate the firm. This is often a root cause for many owner problems.

Under the new paradigm, the compensation system is perceived to be more fair when each owner understands it and knows exactly what he or she must do to in order to earn his or her compensation. This transparency leads to trust and better morale among the owners.

Agreeing Upon Goals

In the old paradigm, goals were not clearly stated. In our 2006 Compensation Survey, we asked the question, "Do owners in your firm have written goals?" Eighty percent responded negatively. If a goal is not written down, how can owners be held accountable? And 74 percent of the firms responding to our survey indicated they had either no evaluation or only an informal evaluation for owners. Only 10 percent of the respondents said they use a formal evaluation method. Under the new model goals are clearly developed and documented at the beginning of the year, and there is mutual agreement between the owner and firm management about the reward. While management may suggest goals to owners, individual owners must take responsibility for them. This requires commitment and buy in. The win-win agreement allows this to happen. Unless owners are involved in setting their goals, there will likely be no commitment to them.

Creating a New Culture

During the Clinton-Bush Presidential race in 1992, the Clinton team came up with a brief but effective winning theme: "It's the economy, Stupid." Our winning theme for the new compensation paradigm is "It's the culture, Stupid." Culture is simply the collective behaviors of everyone in your firm. Albert Einstein is often quoted as saying if you keep doing what you always have done, you will continue to get the same results. In short, if behaviors do not change, you cannot expect different results.

The new paradigm requires an examination and evaluation of the results that are being produced and an exploration of the individual behaviors that are causing those results. Then, you must explore why people behave the way they do. Generally, it is because they have found personal success with these behaviors in the past. When their behaviors, however, do not get the *desired* results, you must explore even more deeply *why* they engage in behaviors that do not get desired results. This is generally due to incomplete or inaccurate beliefs (paradigms). Remember, behaviors will only change when individuals change their beliefs. For example, if as a professional service provider, you believe business development is a noncore or uncomfortable activity, you will likely not engage in business development activities. The results will be pretty evident: very little or no business development.

Exercising Courage

Under the old paradigm, owners were seldom formally evaluated by management. According to the results of our survey, while 81 percent of the respondents believe that owners should have written goals, 80 percent of the firms indicated that their owners do not have any written goals. Because of this, it is extremely difficult to have formal evaluation.

Underperforming owners were often retained because of close friendships or other emotional or subjective reasons. Under the old standard, it was easier for management to simply turn away than to make a hard decision regarding the underperformer. Sadly, both the firm and the individual owner were often dissatisfied. In the new environment, underperformers have no place to hide. They have only three choices: They can (1) accept compensation system changes and strive to increase their performance, (2) be asked to leave the firm, or (3) elect to leave on their own accord. Remaining as an underperformer is no longer an option.

Balancing Individual and Firm Benefits

Too often, under the old model owners focused only on their own enrichment and betterment. As long as they won, they did not care if anyone lost. The goals of each owner were independent rather than interdependent.

The focus of the new compensation model has changed. Firms are moving toward interdependent goals that develop a culture of cooperation, teamwork, and abundance. Studies have shown, and as Stephen R. Covey points out in *The 7 Habits of Highly Effective People*,[4] a philosophy of abundance rather than one of scarcity produces more for everyone.

FINAL THOUGHTS

While your old compensation system may not have been perfect, it had some good points and probably served you well in the old environment. Times are changing, and now is the time to change your views on compensation and income allocation so you can make needed changes to the compensation system. Will the new system be perfect? We doubt it. Your paradigms will always be incomplete.

---

[4]Stephen R. Covey, *The 7 Habits of Highly Effective People* (New York: The Free Press, 2004).

The best advice we can offer you is to identify which of the old paradigms we've described are prevalent in your firm today. They could be standing in the way of growing the compensation pie and using it as a true strategic asset. When you identify the old paradigms as well as the negative effects they are having on your firm, you can begin to make the shift to developing a new and more effective compensation system.

EXHIBIT 1–1   Old Versus New Compensation Paradigms for Owners

Old Compensation Paradigm	*New Compensation Paradigm*
1. Owners measured on same criteria	1. Owners measured on similar criteria, but customized goals
2. Formula/subjective approach	2. Win-win agreement
3. Focus on current production	3. Focus on current production and building future capacity
4. Sink or swim—no support from firm	4. Safety net—firm resources available for success
5. Entitlement compensation system	5. Performance compensation system
6. Guaranteed compensation with small risk	6. Larger at risk compensation
7. Current system perceived as unfair	7. Perceived as fair
8. Goals not understood	8. Owners in agreement over goals
9. Old culture, no changes	9. Firm's culture changing
10. Low performance accepted	10. Low performance recognized and addressed
11. Goals focus on individual performance	11. Goals interdependent, as well

2

HOW TO GROW THE COMPENSATION PIE: THE LEADERSHIP FACTOR

"A leader takes people where they want to go. A great leader takes people where they don't necessarily want to go, but ought to be."

—Rosalynn Carter

Do not bemoan the fact there is shortage of future leaders in your firm. In fact, there is a shortage of leaders not only in the accounting profession, but in corporate America as well. The shortage is not going away, so it will be up to you to identify and develop new leaders.

You may be wondering what it takes to be a successful leader in today's rapidly changing, often confusing, and intensely competitive environment. To that end, you may want to throw out what you currently believe about leadership and what you currently believe leaders do. A challenge for most accounting firm leaders, however, is they have a lot invested in the past. They got to their current positions because they did incredibly well at yesterday's activities. One common characteristic of unsuccessful leaders is that they are often committed to outdated strategies and ideas. "Anyone who believes that anything they have done in the last 20 years makes any sense at all compared to the next 20 years should not even be in a position of leadership," argues management guru Tom Peters.

Take a minute or so and ask yourself the following questions to determine your readiness to become a more effective leader:

- Am I operating based on new beliefs?
- Am I moving the firm's strategic vision ahead?
- Do I challenge the status quo?
- Am I willing to let go of the past?
- Do I rethink my basic assumptions about the firm, its competitors, and the market?
- Do I understand what makes a good leader?
- Do my fellow owners challenge my leadership techniques?
- Have I changed my leadership beliefs in the last five years?

If you answered no to three or more of the above questions, you are likely committed to old beliefs. The first step in growing the compensation pie is becoming a real leader in the firm.

This chapter discusses what it takes to be a leader, what leaders do, and how to be a leader.

WHAT IT TAKES TO BE A LEADER

There has been much research on what it takes to be a leader, and you will find countless sources to support any one of the many positions. There are those who argue that great leaders are born (the personality theorists), and there are those who observe leaders in terms of task-orientation and relation-orientation (the behavioral theorists). Strong leadership has also been seen to depend on adjusting one's style to the styles of others. Most recently, principle-centered leadership has become the hallmark of sound leadership.[1] Peter Drucker perhaps captured the essence of leadership when he wrote, "Management is doing things right; leadership is doing the right things."

Robert W. Terry, the author of *Authentic Leadership: Courage in Action*, notes, "Leadership is not to be reduced to techniques, quick fixes, or heroics. It is to be viewed as a particular mode of engagement with life, requiring a lifelong commitment to growing toward human fulfillment."

WHAT LEADERS DO

The day of the autocratic and hierarchical leadership styles and methods no longer work in today's professional environment. While there are countless things that leaders do every day, we have identified, based on our work with hundreds of firms, seven key activities that make for successful leadership.

Leaders Create a Shared Vision

No matter where you want to go in life, you need a vision, a point of arrival. In *Alice's Adventures in Wonderland*, Alice asked the Cheshire Cat, "Would you tell me please which way I ought to go from here?" The Cat responded, "That depends on where you want to get to." Alice then said, "I don't much care where." And as the Cat told Alice, "Then it doesn't matter which way you go."

There should be little debate about the significance of vision. It is virtually impossible for any firm or business to operate without one. Joanne G. Sujansky, Ph.D., the founder of KEYGroup® and the author of six books, including *The Keys to Mastering Leadership*, observes in "Keys to Unlocking Leadership in Your Organization" that "Dynamic leaders consistently develop, articulate and reverberate from a clear, concrete and inspiring vision. They draw out natural desire and build unity and momentum through an exciting and colorful picture of possibility."[2]

---

[1]For more on this topic, see *Principle Centered Leadership* by Stephen R. Covey (New York: Simon & Schuster, 1991).

[2]Joanne G. Sujansky, "Keys to Unlocking Leadership in Your Organization," *Partner Advantage Advisory*, vol. 2, no. 7, p.6.

Vision is not just for the leader. Employees need to know where the firm is headed. Does the firm want to win the championship or perform well in the race, or does it just want to be a mediocre player? Without clear direction, firm leaders and employees surely flounder. They must see the big picture. If they cannot, there is little motivation and congruence. Employees are motivated by a vivid sense of the future. They like to work for what could be, not what is. Sam Allred, founder of Upstream Academy, helps firms capture the essence of vision when he asks firm leaders to paint a picture of what the future would look like to owners, employees, and clients over time. It is when people can see and are committed to the vision that they are able to accomplish great things. Perhaps the greatest national vision during the past 100 years was created on May 25, 1961, by President John F. Kennedy in a speech to a Joint Session of Congress about his vision of landing a man on the moon and returning him safely to earth.

> I believe we possess all the resources and talents necessary. But the facts of the matter are that we have never made the national decisions or marshaled the national resources required for such leadership. We have never specified long-range goals on an urgent time schedule, or managed our resources and our time as to insure their fulfillment. . . .
>
> This decision demands a major national commitment of scientific and technical manpower, material and facilities, and the possibility of their diversion from other important activities where they are already thinly spread. It means a degree of dedication, organization, and discipline which have not always characterized our research and development efforts.

Before we leave the topic of leaders creating a shared vision, we invite you to consider the following questions:

- What is your personal guiding vision?
- What is the guiding vision for your firm?
- How do you describe that vision to others?
- Will everyone be able to tell when you reach it?
- What will it mean to you and other owners if and when you reach it?
- What will it mean to employees?
- What will it mean to clients?

Certainly, President Kennedy's vision of space exploration created an exciting and colorful picture of possibility. Does your firm's current vision articulate a clear and inspiring future?

Leaders Make Things Happen

Peter Drucker, in *The Leader of the Future*, observes that "An effective leader is not someone who is loved or admired. He or she is someone whose followers do the right thing. Popularity is not leadership. Results are."[3] Essentially, a leader is someone others choose to follow. To get results and to influence people to choose to follow, successful leaders often

---

[3] Frances Hesselbein, Marshall Goldsmith, and Richard Beckhard, *The Leader of the Future* (San Francisco: Jossey-Bass. 1996).

take risks, and they do so with visibility and vulnerability. Vulnerability permits them to be open about their weaknesses, fears, and behavior. Leaders grow and develop through action.

Leaders Take Ownership

True leaders understand the firm must continue to evolve—to grow and change—and the journey from where they are to where they want to be is often as daunting as a trip to the moon. Hence, effective leaders lead change initiatives by taking overall ownership of the desired changes and managing both the barriers that get in the way and the stress that accompanies any change initiative. Good leaders also take complete responsibility for their own decisions and actions. When things go wrong, they do not blame others and excuse themselves. When things go right, they share credit with others rather than taking it themselves.

This is especially true when changing or modifying a compensation system.

Leaders Build Teams

Leaders realize they cannot do it by themselves. And one can only be a positional leader if he or she has followers. Effective leaders surround themselves with owners and team members with different perspectives, talents, and interests. This diversity of talent and perspective is necessary to drive change in an organization.

Building teams is one way of unlocking your leadership potential. Your firm is certainly a team, but you may also have niche teams, service teams, engagement teams, and specialty teams, among others.

This is where the well-known practice of using mistakes as learning opportunities provides a key to unlocking talent. Winning leaders encourage team members to take calculated risks, to pick themselves up when these risks don't "pan out," and to use mistakes as learning opportunities. When people know that mistakes are understood as a part of our experience, they will be more creative, take more risks, and become stronger and more adept in the process.

We believe effective leaders also become masterful coaches. They not only endeavor to develop and improve their coaching skills, but they also benefit from being coached. They become masterful listeners to ensure they understand others and become keen observers to ensure they catch people succeeding and openly praise them.

Leaders Motivate by Modeling

Leaders must first learn to lead themselves before they can lead others. They must model to motivate. Successful leaders motivate others not only by communicating shared vision but also by their own consistent behavior and principles.

While successful leaders often exhibit a high degree of integrity, authenticity, courage, and curiosity, they create trust. We prefer Patrick

Lencioni's definition of trust as found in his work *Overcoming the Five Dysfunctions of a Team*: "Trust is not the ability of team members to predict one another's behaviors because they've known each other for a long time." He adds, "Trust is all about vulnerability. . . . Vulnerability-based trust is predicated on the simple and practical idea that people who aren't afraid to admit the truth about themselves are not going to engage in the kind of political behavior that wastes everyone's time and energy, and more important, makes the accomplishment of results an unlikely scenario."[4]

Leaders Look Behind the Numbers

Don't get us wrong. The numbers are important. They serve as a reality check; they allow you to see if you are on course. And while your fellow owners may judge you by the numbers you deliver, leaders realize there is more to running a firm than simply looking at the numbers from time to time.

Numbers alone may measure a firm's short-term success, but they are not a true measure of the firm's long-term success. Many examples prove this, and the grand-daddy of all is Enron. In his 2003 article entitled, "Rethinking the Leadership Agenda," author Rowan Gibson cites noted strategist Al Ries as saying, "A company being run by the numbers is a company being run into the ground."

Instead of creating genuine growth by developing a meaningful and sustainable strategy for wealth creation, many leaders do everything they can to create an illusion of growth. They may reduce staff, cut costs, and look for efficiencies in business processes. Almost no one, however, has built a sustainable business by cutting costs.

Today's general business culture suggests a fanatic obsession with financial results, but a leader's focus should be on, as Stephen R. Covey put it, "Focusing on results today in a way that helps us get even better results in the future." It should be on creating a brilliant and differentiated competitive strategy for the firm—one that has well-aligned systems, structures, and processes to support it.

Leaders Observe and Listen

Leaders watch what is going on in the environment. Leaders also listen to anyone and everyone, including fellow owners and employees, clients, competitors, and leaders in other industries. They know this informal feedback system is critical for long-term success and effectiveness. By listening, they often make better decisions because they learn more about those things that drive results (driving forces) and those things that get in the way of goal accomplishment (restraining forces).

---

[4]Patrick Lencioni, *Overcoming the Five Dysfunctions of a Team: A Leadership Fable* (San Francisco: Jossey-Bass. 2005), p. 13-14.

HOW TO BE A LEADER

In its workshop The 4 Roles of Leadership, the FranklinCovey Company categorizes many of the activities previously described into four key roles that leaders play: pathfinding, aligning, empowering, and modeling.

In pathfinding, the leader helps all members of the firm understand the internal and external environment; identify and prioritize client, employee, and other stakeholder needs; and execute strategies to meet those needs.

In aligning, the leader develops organizational work processes, structures, and enabling systems to support effective strategies.

In empowering, the leader creates conditions that enable and support all employees in contributing their maximum potential to fulfilling the mission. Great leaders recognize gender differences and generational differences in the workforce and realize they must allow the future workforce to be involved in painting the new picture of accounting firm leadership.

In modeling, the leader establishes trust by walking the talk; setting the example of character and competence; and living the firm's mission, vision, and values.

Another key to successful and enduring leadership is resilience—the ability to bounce back from crises, sudden or continuous changes, and the intense demands of today's organizations. One of the most important things you can do to improve resilience is to have good physical health. There is nothing new about the importance of good nutrition, sufficient rest, and meaningful playtime. Leaders live with great challenges and demands; the ones that ride the whitewater of today's business world with composure maintain their reserves and make energy withdrawals without breaking the bank.

You do not need to be a rocket scientist to develop leadership skills. And while it is a fairly straightforward undertaking, it is not easy. It requires true commitment and real effort every day. In "Five Steps to Becoming a Stronger Leader: A Challenge for 2004," Morrie Shechtman noted, "As you may have come to suspect, embracing the hard work required to become a better leader will not just affect your life at the office. The changes wrought by following these principles will 'spill over' into your personal relationships as well. That's a good thing. What you do for a living is an organic extension of who you are, and vice versa. If you compartmentalize, you compromise your core values."[5]

FINAL THOUGHTS

Not many consultants relate firm leadership and execution with owner compensation. But without effective leadership there would be no profits to distribute. One of management's overriding responsibilities is to increase owner value.

If you do not grow as a leader, you are choosing to settle for mediocrity. That may get you by for a short time, but it will not carry you through

---

[5]Morrie Shechtman, "Five Steps to Becoming a Stronger Leader: A Challenge for 2004," *Partner Advantage Advisory*, vol. 1, no. 7, p. 8.

the whitewater that lies ahead. Real leaders constantly diagnose the situation, then design, develop, and implement solutions. This includes how compensation is determined. Today's leaders focus on both the now (current production) and the future (building production capacity) and reward accordingly.

To drive above average results, successful leaders clarify expectations and tasks, and build strong and trusting relationships with other owners. There is no more powerful way for gaining commitment, building loyalty, and strengthening the firm. Yet, as with vision, it is not enough to simply clarify and articulate expectations. It is necessary to set goals and specific targets so that success can be easily identified, measured and rewarded.

3

GROWING THE COMPENSATION PIE: THE BIG PICTURE FACTOR

"All organizations are perfectly aligned to get the results they get."

—Jim Stuart

No matter how noble or powerful your organizational mission (why your firm exists), that mission (and your long-term vision) cannot be achieved unless you understand the ecosystem that supports it. To achieve your desired results, you must be clear not only about who you are, who you serve, and why but also how you do so. You must create organizational alignment.

Organizational alignment is linking strategy, systems and processes, people and culture, to best accomplish the mission, vision, and desired business results of an organization. Alignment occurs when the above elements are mutually supportive and focused on effective and efficient delivery of results.

The first step is an understanding of *why* organizations get the good results they get and why they get the not-so-good results they get—and it's *not* based on their compensation criteria or methodology. This chapter discusses two organizational models important to accounting firms: the 7S Model and the Organizational Effectiveness Model.

THE 7S MODEL

While employed as a client partner and business developer at FranklinCovey Co., Coral received her first exposure to the company's performance cycle, later to be called the Organizational Effectiveness Cycle (OEC). She came to understand it as an iteration of McKinsey's "7S" Model, which illustrates the seven key components of an organization, which is charted in Exhibit 3–1, "The 7S Model." The 7S-Model was developed by Tom Peters, Robert Waterman, and Julien R. Phillips, consultants at McKinsey & Co. They first published the 7S Model in their 1980 article, "Structure Is Not Organization." The model maintains that an organization is not just its structure, but it consists of seven distinct elements, three of which are dubbed "hard" and four of which are dubbed "soft."

The three hard S elements—strategy, structure and systems—are tangible and easy to identify. They can be found in a firm's strategy statements, business plans, organizational charts, and other documentation. The four soft S elements—skills, staff, shared values, and style—are intangible. They are difficult to describe since capabilities, values, and elements of your firm's culture are continuously developing and changing. The soft elements are highly determined by the people who work in the organization. Therefore, it is much more difficult to plan or to influence the characteristics of the soft elements. Although the soft factors are intangible, they have a significant impact on the hard strategy, structure, and systems of the organization.

Peters, Waterman, and Phillips describe the Seven S's as follows:[1]

The Hard Ss	
Strategy	Actions an organization takes in light of changes in its external environment
Structure	Basis for specialization and coordination influenced primarily by strategy and by organization size and diversity
Systems	Formal and informal procedures that support the strategy and structure
The Soft Ss	
Style and culture	The culture of the organization, consisting of two components:
	Organizational culture: The dominant values, beliefs, and norms that develop over time and become relatively enduring features of organizational life
	Management style: more a matter of what managers do than what they say; how they spend their time
Staff	The people and human resource management processes used to develop managers, shape basic values of management cadre, introduce recruits to the company, manage the careers of employees
Skills	The distinctive competences—what the firm does best and what individuals do best
Shared values	Guiding concepts, fundamental ideas around which a business is built

As in nature, all organizations have their own ecosystems in which each element has its place yet is dependent on the other elements for long-term survival. Effective organizations maintain a fine balance between and among the seven Ss.

---

[1]Tom Peters, Robert Waterman, and Julien R. Phillips, *In Search of Excellence: Lessons from America's Best Run Companies* (New York: Warner Books, 1982), p. 9-11.

APPLYING THE 7S ELEMENTS TO ACCOUNTING FIRMS

Let's take a look at how this might work in an accounting firm. Following is a description of the seven Ss in a public accounting firm.

The Hard Ss	
Strategy	Actions a firm takes in light of regulatory, technological, economic, or social changes that effect the accounting profession, the firm, or the firm's clients
Structure	The way the firm is organized (e.g., departments, niches, service groups, and work teams) and the way work flows through the firm
Systems	Formal and informal processes and procedures that support the strategy and structure
The Soft Ss	
Style and culture	The culture of the firm consisting of two components:
	Organizational culture: the dominant values, beliefs, and norms that develop over time and become relatively enduring features of organizational life
	Management style: how firm leaders behave on a daily basis
Staff	The people and human resource management processes:
	■ Recruitment and selection
	■ Orientation and onboarding
	■ Mentoring and coaching
	■ Learning and development
	■ Performance management
	■ Compensation
Skills	The distinctive competencies of the firm and of each individual within the firm
Shared values	Guiding concepts, fundamental ideas around which the firm is built—how individuals within the firm treat each other and how they treat clients and other key stakeholders

If one of the seven elements changes, each of the other elements is affected. For example, a change in human resource systems such as internal career plans and management training, will have an impact on organizational culture (management style), and thus will affect structures, processes, and finally characteristic competences of the organization.

According to Dagmar Recklies, when firms try to make changes, they usually focus their efforts on the hard Ss—strategy, structure, and systems—believing these are easier to change. "If we change our strategy," says one managing owner, "won't we get different results?" Traditionally, this has been the approach public accounting firms have taken when starting a change process. Unfortunately, however, it is the wrong place to start.

Most companies and public accounting firms care less for the soft Ss—skills, staff, style, and shared values. Peters and Waterman in *In Search of Excellence* observed that most successful companies work hard at these soft Ss.[2] Few companies, including public accounting firms, have taken their advice to heart. We know that soft factors can make or break a change process, since new structures and strategies are difficult to build when the culture is dysfunctional or values are not shared. The dissatisfying results of most mergers, whether small or spectacular mega-mergers, are often based on a clash of completely different cultures, values, and styles, which makes it difficult to establish effective, common systems and structures.

THE ORGANIZATIONAL EFFECTIVENESS CYCLE (OEC)

Like the 7S Model, the OEC (Exhibit 3–2) helps us see our organizations in a holistic fashion, and if properly employed, it can be a powerful instrument to help leaders increase performance and achieve sustainable results. The OEC reorganizes the elements of the 7S Model and serves as two leadership tools:

1. A *graphic model*, which illustrates the relationships among all key components of an organization and defines the path for leading change in a firm, department, or functional area.
2. A *methodology*, which enables leaders to diagnose root causes and to design root solutions systematically and effectively—and answer the question, "How can we develop a more highly effective firm?"

The Organizational Effectiveness Cycle as a Graphic Model

To illustrate the relationships among all key components of an organization, we must first know the components. They are:

- Customer and other stakeholder needs (other stakeholders may be internal or external and may include employees and their family members, vendors and suppliers, community members, and shareholders, among others).
- Mission (why we exist), vision (where we are going), and values (how we will treat each other along the way). (Chapter 4 offers a detailed discussion on mission, vision, and core values.)
- Strategy (how we accomplish the goals of the organization).
- Systems and processes (how work flows and is accomplished on a day-to-day basis). Examples may include accounts payable and accounts receivable processes, training/systems, performance management, compensation systems, and the way a tax return is processed.
- Organizational culture (the collective behaviors of an organization's members).
- Results we are trying to accomplish for internal and/or external stakeholders.

---

[2]Peters, Waterman, and Phillips, p. 9-11.

Exhibit 3–2, "Organizational Effectiveness Cycle," illustrates the components of the OEC. When used as a model for leading change, we start by "seeking first to understand" what our key stakeholders want and need from us. Continuing clockwise on the model, we move to mission. Our organization exists, then, based on what we hear from our key stakeholders, to meet as many of those wants and needs as we can, given our collective skill and desire. Rallying the troops to fulfill client wants and needs is where vision comes in.

In his book *Leading Change*, John P. Kotter shares eight reasons that major change efforts often fail.[3] Three of them have to do with vision: underestimating the power of vision, undercommunicating the vision, and permitting obstacles to block the vision. First, without a sound vision, the "paperless" initiative, the new niche team structure, the revised 360-degree performance appraisal system, the pay-for-performance compensation, and bonus system may not be taken seriously or implemented properly.

Second, Kotter believes major change is usually impossible unless most employees are willing to help, often to the point of making short-term sacrifices. Without credible communication, and a lot of it, he says, employees' hearts and minds are never captured. Finally, the implementation of the vision requires action (individual and collective behaviors) from everyone. Even though employees may be behind the vision, however, they often experience roadblocks in the form of firm strategy (for example, they do not know what it is), firm structure (for example, the way teams and departments are organized), or people systems (for example, compensation or performance appraisal systems that force people to choose between the noble goal and their self-interests, supervisors that demand behaviors that are counter to the vision, employees who get away with dysfunctional behaviors because supervisors lack the courage to deal with them, or hiring people for their strong technical skills only).

Many firm leaders believe the owner retreat (often called the strategic planning retreat) should "fix" things—that results should change because we have changed the strategic plan. While strategy development is important, the OEC framework suggests people (not strategy) are the key to results and change. So, if we want a change in results, we must get different behaviors from employees—which inherently means a change in the systems that recognize and develop their knowledge and skills or that motivate their behavior.

So, after defining strategy, leaders are responsible for designing effective and efficient processes and systems that allow people to work together synergistically. And it is what people do (or do not do) on a daily basis that gets results (that is, change).

The Organizational Effectiveness Cycle as a Methodology

When using the OEC as a model for leading change, you "work" the model in a clockwise fashion, beginning with stakeholder needs. However, when

---

[3]John P. Kotter, *Leading Change* (Boston: Harvard Business School Publishing, 1996).

using the OEC as a methodology for diagnosing root causes and designing root solutions, you "work" the model in a counter-clockwise fashion.

To diagnose why you are not getting the measurable results you want (for example, revenue, profitability, realization, employee retention, and client satisfaction scores), you must look at what people are (and are not) doing to get those results. What behaviors do you need more of, and what behaviors do you need less of?

Then, you must ask yourself, "Why do people do (or not do) those things?" This generally leads you to one or more of three answers:

1. They do not know what to do (know-what).
2. They do not know how to do it (know-how).
3. They are not motivated to do it (know-why).

As a result, you are forced to look at *why* they don't know what, how, or why. And it almost always boils down to an ineffective system (for example, hiring system, training system, performance management system, compensation system, or information system) or ineffective structure (for example, team formation, wrong people in the right place, or right people in the wrong place).

This forces you to ask much bigger questions. They include:

- "Why did we organize ourselves this way?"
- "Why did we hire people who don't share the same values we share?"
- "Why don't people have the skills they need to allow us to leverage more effectively?"
- "Why don't managers and owners delegate more work?"
- "Why did we accept client(s) that are inconsistent with our acceptance standards?"

The answers to these questions tell you what's wrong with the systems and structures you currently have in place and how they are holding you and your employees back.

FINAL THOUGHTS

Again, it's not strategy that gets results—especially financial results. It's people that get them. So, your ability to continue your noble mission by sustaining and improving margins compels you to focus on people (a soft S), to identify and outline the behaviors that are needed to produce your desired results, and to build systems that help people engage in those behaviors. Why? Because all organizations are perfectly aligned to get the results they get.

Few firms will achieve complete alignment. The goal is simply a degree of compatibility and consistency that lets people devote their energy toward accomplishing results, with a minimum of effort toward overcoming obstacles.

EXHIBIT 3–1 The 7S Model[4]

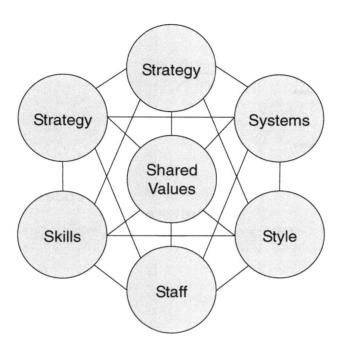

[4]Reprinted from *Business Horizons*, Volume 23, Issue 3, Robert Waterman, Thomas Peters, and Julien Phillips, "Structure is Not Organization," Pages 14-26, Copyright, June 1980, with permission from Elsevier.

EXHIBIT 3–2   Organizational Effectiveness Cycle[5]

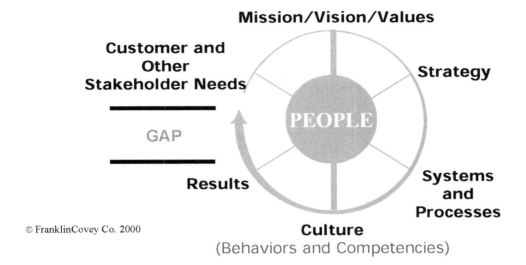

© FranklinCovey Co. 2000

4

HOW TO GROW THE COMPENSATION PIE: THE MISSION/VISION/VALUES FACTOR

"Leadership is about change. It's about taking people from where they are now to where they need to be. The best way to get people to venture into unknown terrain is to make it desirable by taking them there in their imaginations."

—Noel M. Tichy

Firms that maximize profits usually have close alignment amongst mission, vision, values, strategy, and systems, especially the compensation system. If you are concerned at all about driving financial results in your firm, you will eventually need to align owner and employee compensation to the firm's strategic initiatives.

Before we get into a discussion about tying compensation to the firm's strategic initiatives, however, it is necessary to have a clear understanding of three critical components of the Organizational Effectiveness Cycle introduced in Chapter 3: mission, vision, and values.

Strategic alignment cannot be achieved unless owners and employees know what to align themselves with. That is why mission (why you exist), vision (where you are going), and core values (how you will treat each other along the way) are so critical to the strategic success of a firm and why they need to be considered when designing an effective compensation system. This is shown in Exhibit 4–1, "The Profitable Firm's Foundation."

This chapter discusses how a firm establishes its mission, vision, and values.

DETERMINING MISSION AND VISION

When we facilitate owner strategic planning retreats, we are often asked by one or several owners, "Why are we wasting time talking about mission and vision?" At that point we ask them to write down the firm's mission and vision.

The responses are usually wide and varied. Most everyone has a different take on why the firm is in business (mission) and what it wants to become (vision). For example, "We want to be the best firm in the market" or "We offer the highest quality service." Even when a firm has a written mission, almost no one can remember it. In short, it likely doesn't mean much, and therefore, doesn't drive individual or collective behavior.

Mission

Gertrude Stein, an American writer, poet, feminist, playwright, and catalyst in the development of modern art and literature, said, "It is awfully important to know what is and what is not your business." So, let's start with defining mission and exploring how to develop one.

First, a mission tells everyone inside and outside the firm why you do what you do and why the firm exists. In short, it provides the organization's reason for being.

Peter Drucker says the mission should "fit on a T-shirt," yet a mission statement is not a slogan. It is a precise statement of purpose. Words should be chosen for their meaning rather than beauty, for their clarity over cleverness. The best missions have plain speech with no technical jargon and no adornments.[1]

The mission, as Drucker notes, should be a concise statement of the firm's business strategy and developed from the customer's perspective, not the firm's perspective, for example, "The mission is broad, even eternal, yet directs you to do the right things now and into the future so that everyone in the organization can say, 'What I am doing contributes to the goal.'"[2]

As we mentioned earlier in this chapter, public accounting firm owners often have misguided ideas about the answer to why their firm exists. For example, when we ask the question, "Why does this firm exist?" owners usually provide the following answers:

- To make a profit
- To provide quality service
- To be number one in the market
- To be recognized as a leader in our market
- To provide opportunities for staff

Most initial responses are internally focused and rarely touch upon the real reason the firm exists—the real or psychological needs, or both, that are fulfilled when customers buy your products and services.

Firms do not have a *right* to exist. They exist only because they provide services or products to a market that needs these services and products. Hence, a more appropriate answer to the question "Why does the firm exist?" might read as follows:

- To actively identify operational opportunities that help small business clients succeed.
- To understand our clients' financial goals and then help them to achieve them.
- To provide workable technology solutions to manufacturers.

---

[1]Peter Drucker, *The Drucker Foundation Self-Assessment Tool: Process Guide* (San Francisco: Jossey-Bass, 1999).
[2]Drucker, p. 15.

- To be the outsourced controller and bookkeeper for small businesses.
- To help our clients achieve their personal financial goals through solid investment advice.

When you create or revise the firm's mission, consider the firm's core clients, existing service offerings and products, geographic markets, and competition. It's also best to involve as many people in its creation as possible. A brainstorming session with owners and select employees is an excellent way to get started.

So, how will you know you created a good mission, one that hasn't been watered down? Here is a brief list of questions to help you:

- Is it short and sharply focused so everyone in the firm can remember it?
- Is it clear and easily understood?
- Does it say why the firm exists?
- Is it broad enough?
- Does it inspire owner and employee commitment?
- Does it illustrate what the firm wants to be remembered for?

Dynamic missions take time to develop since you are trying to capture the essence of the firm in just a few words. It *can* be done, and it is definitely worth the effort. We can only imagine how much time was spent by the International Red Cross in developing its mission statement: "Serve the most vulnerable." Take a minute to review the above questions in our checklist against the Red Cross's mission. You will see the power of a well-drafted mission.

Vision

August J. Aquila and Bruce Marcus, in *Client at the Core: Marketing and Managing Today's Professional Services Firm*, best capture the concept of a vision: "There is no concept so dangerous as one that appears the most simple. . . . Most firm managers have an idea of where they want to take their firms. The danger is that they call that idea a *vision*, without really being able to articulate it. They hang it on a rack, like an old coat, and forget about it." The authors add, "[A vision is] valuable if it isn't a vague, unarticulated dream (*'I'd like to have the biggest firm in the region'*), or if it's not based in reality (*'My partner and I would like to be global by this time next year'*.) A vision isn't a wish, or something that can be made to come true by waving a wand."[3]

A vision is a useful management tool if there's a blueprint to accomplish it. It's useful if it's realistic, and if you're willing to take the arduous and meticulous steps to make it a reality. It's a guide to developing a business plan—and a marketing plan—that accomplishes the vision.

A good vision is an articulated description of your firm's desired future. Note the emphasis on the future; the vision isn't true today and it describes your firm as you'd like it to be in, say, five, ten, or more years, and fulfilling it is an ongoing process.

---

[3]August J. Aquila and Bruce Marcus, *Client at the Core: Marketing and Managing Today's Professional Services Firm* (Hoboken, N.J.: John Wiley and Sons, 2004), p. 41.

Since clients don't really care about your vision, it should be an internal document. If your vision is to become a regional accounting firm, clients who need a regional accounting firm to serve their needs won't likely be interested in you today. They may say or just have the attitude, "Contact us when you become a regional accounting firm."

Vision creates excitement and passion in people. It paints the future. All of us have had visions in our lifetimes. Young men and women have visions of becoming doctors, astronauts, scientists, lawyers, and accountants. Almost every owner in a public accounting firm started with a vision of becoming an owner and then worked toward fulfilling it.

It is said that Nike's original vision was "Crush Adidas." Adidas was the number one sport shoe maker at the time. Everyone at Nike knew what they were working for, and they knew what success would look like.

As we mentioned in Chapter 2, President John F. Kennedy, in 1961, created perhaps one of the century's most important visions when he said, "I believe that this nation should commit itself to achieving the goal, before this decade is out, of landing a man on the moon, and returning him safely to earth."

In addition to the checklist in Chapter 2, the following items can also help you evaluate the effectiveness of your vision:

- Do all employees understand the firm's vision?
- Does the vision promote a sense of "oh wow"?
- Does everyone know how they help the firm achieve its vision?
- Does the vision motivate all employees to do their best?
- Can owners and employees visualize what their life becomes when the firm achieves its vision?

After clearly defining mission and vision, you are ready to identify, define, and describe core values. These are the behaviors that are acceptable in your firm—how you will treat each other and your key stakeholders along the way.

DEVELOPING VALUES

Values, including how you and others behave in accordance with them, determine the firm's culture. Values are critically important when creating strategic alignment and designing an effective compensation system.

We follow a three-step process when helping firms develop their values: identify the values, define the values, and describe the values.

Step 1. Identify the Values

Establish four to six core values the firm will embrace. Many firms consider values that relate to client service, shareholders, employees, and the community. Examples may include community involvement, teamwork, integrity, or continuous improvement. Ensure all team members can identify the difference between the firm's preferred values and its actual values today.

Step 2. Define the Values

Ask all team members to define in 10 to 12 words what each core value means to them. All responses should be taken into consideration, and an assimilation should result in a 12- to 20-word definition.

Step 3. Describe the Values

Invite employees to describe specific behaviors that represent each core value. Ask employees and owners to provide behavioral examples of how each core value is lived in the firm and what it would look like if people were doing so. These behaviors become the criteria against which individuals will be evaluated and on which a portion of their compensation will be determined.

FINAL THOUGHTS

Here is a simple way to determine where your firm stands relative to a real mission and vision as well as values by which people can live. At the end of an owner's meeting ask each owner to document answers to the following questions.

- Do we have a single vision for this firm?
- Can every one in the firm clearly state it in 25 words or less?
- Do we have one firm culture or many cultures in the firm? If so, why? If not, why not?
- Have we identified the three or four most important goals the firm needs to accomplish this year?
- If so, how many people in the firm know what they are?
- Have we identified what success in each one of these goals means and looks like? If not, when will we do so? If so, what is it?
- On a scale of 1 to 10, how motivated and committed are (1) the owners and (2) the staff to achieving these goals?
- What has to happen during the next 12 months to achieve the goals?

Then, at the following owner's meeting, distribute the collective responses. The gathered data will make for robust and dynamic dialogue. Remember, mission, vision, and values are the foundation upon which every profitable firm is built. Firms without them lack clear direction and guiding principles, and firms whose leaders have carefully defined them and execute based *on* them are positioned for long-term success and profitability.

We also hold that clarity of mission, vision, and values form the foundation for building an effective compensation system. Owners and employees should be rewarded first for doing the right things. The right things are those activities that fulfill the firm's vision, live its mission, and reflect the firm's core values. Doing the right things lead to superior performance. And since it's performance that counts, performance should also be rewarded.

EXHIBIT 4–1   The Profitable Firm's Foundation

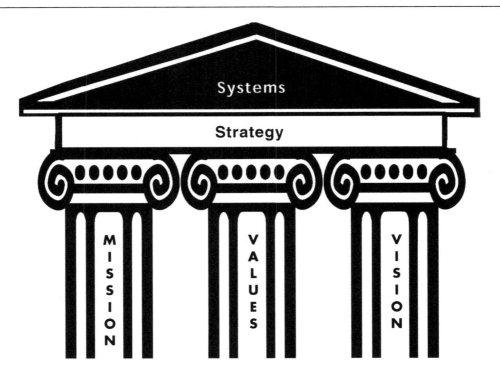

5

HOW TO GROW THE COMPENSATION PIE: THE BALANCED SCORECARD FACTOR[1]

"The general who wins the battle makes many calculations in his temple before the battle is fought. The general who loses makes but few calculations beforehand."

—San Tzu

In Chapter 4, we discuss the critical importance of having a dynamic mission, vision, and set of values as the foundation for long-term success. After you build the foundation, you can start building and managing the firm for profits. Perhaps one of the best modern tools to help manage the firm for profits is the Balanced Scorecard.

In this chapter, we explain the Balanced Scorecard and how to use it successfully in managing a public accounting firm. We also cover how to create strategies and strategy maps.

THE BALANCED SCORECARD

The Balanced Scorecard was created in the early 1990s by Harvard Business School Professor Robert S. Kaplan and consultant David P. Norton, president of Renaissance Solutions, Inc. The Balanced Scorecard was originally developed to measure performance for corporations, especially manufacturing firms. It is now being used in accounting, consulting, and law firms as well as financial institutions and other service-related firms to help implement strategy, monitor objectives, and reward for performance.

While a great deal has been written about the Balanced Scorecard, an important thing to remember is that it measures the results of management's efforts and the effectiveness of management's strategies. In short, it demonstrates how well management is executing strategies and how well people in the firm are achieving their objectives. The Balanced Scorecard is an effective tool that can be used to measure a firm's overall

---

[1]Much of this chapter is based on material originally published in *Client at the Core: Marketing and Managing Today's Professional Services Firm* by August J. Aquila and Bruce W. Marcus (Hoboken, N.J.: John Wiley & Sons, 2004). Adapted with permission of John Wiley & Sons, Inc.

progress, a separate department, an industry team or individual in reaching its goals.

Creating and Selecting Strategies

For the scorecard to work in a professional services firm, owners must first agree upon the firm's mission and vision as well as the strategy or strategies to achieve the mission and reach the vision. That's why we talked in detail about mission, vision, and values in Chapter 4. We now discuss basic concepts of strategies and strategic development.

According to Kaplan and Norton, "An organization's strategy describes how it intends to create value for its shareholders, customers and citizens."[2] A strategy is nothing more than a series of assumptions about what might happen in the future if certain things happen in the present. A firm may assume there are exceptional opportunities by developing a financial services arm. Its strategy may be to grow this part of the practice through acquisition of a handful of independent financial services firms in its market. Until the firm acquires these other practices and integrates them into its culture, it will not know how well the strategy will work or what changes need to be made to clarifying the strategy. The firm may also decide to use short-term strategies, such as reducing costs of service delivery by taking advantage of new technologies.

For 50 years, consumer and business-to-business firms have developed growth strategies for their products and services based on Ansoff's Product/Market Expansion Grid.[3] The following chart is adapted from Ansoff's 1957 grid:

	Current Services	*New Services*
Current Markets	1. Market penetration or client development strategies	2. Service development or cross-servicing strategies
New Markets	3. Market development strategies	4. Diversification strategies

1. Market penetration or client development strategies are based on the assumption that the firm's growth can best be achieved by providing existing services to new clients that are similar to existing clients. These strategies involve the least amount of risk because growth depends on seeking out new clients from markets you already serve and with which you are familiar. For example, a firm with a niche in auto dealerships may decide to expand throughout the state or region.
2. Service development has one known and one unknown element. The known element is existing clients. The unknown element is the new service or product you plan to develop. For example, a local firm with

[2]Robert S. Kaplan and David P. Norton, *Strategy Maps: Converting Intangible Assets into Tangible Outcome* (Boston: Harvard Business School Press, 2004), p. 4.
[3]H. Igor Ansoff, "Strategies for Diversification," *Harvard Business Review* (September/October 1957).

several law firms as consulting clients may decide to start a litigation support service, or a firm may develop a valuation practice to service its closely held business clients.

3. Market development strategies assume firm growth will come by promoting current services to new markets. For example, a firm may develop a strong estate planning practice for physicians and believe there are also opportunities to offer these services to dentists.

4. The most difficult strategies to implement are the diversification strategies because there are two unknowns: the new service or product and a potential new market. The firm may be unfamiliar with the potential clients and lack the requisites to offer the service.

After developing a list of possible strategies, firms must select those that are right for the firm. When selecting strategies, consider the following four questions:

1. Does the strategy fit the firm?
2. Does the firm have sufficient resources to support the strategy?
3. Do the economics of the strategy make sense?
4. How strongly will owners and employees support the strategy?

Gaining Strategic Consensus

Just like vision and mission, it is of critical importance for owners to gain consensus on the firm's strategy—that is, how the firm will realize its goals. Without this initial agreement, it's almost impossible for the firm to move ahead in a unified fashion. Gaining strategic consensus is the first step in building individual owner involvement, commitment, and accountability in a firm. Once the strategic consensus is reached, owners and other key firm personnel must then develop objectives, measures, targets, and tasks since they share a common viewpoint.

Employing the Balanced Scorecard to Implement Strategy

Public accounting firm owners often leave strategic planning meetings and retreats confused about how they intend to achieve overall firm objectives.

While the Balanced Scorecard does not create the firm's strategies, it does help owners and employees understand how they will execute their strategies by monitoring and measuring four critical areas or perspectives that create value for the firm:

- Financial
- Clients
- Internal systems and business processes
- Employee growth and learning

Some firms add areas such as marketing. The chart below shows the key objectives in a professional services firm. Let's briefly examine these four areas and how they are interrelated. (Please see Chapter 10 for a discussion of specific objectives that firms may wish to accomplish in each of these key areas).

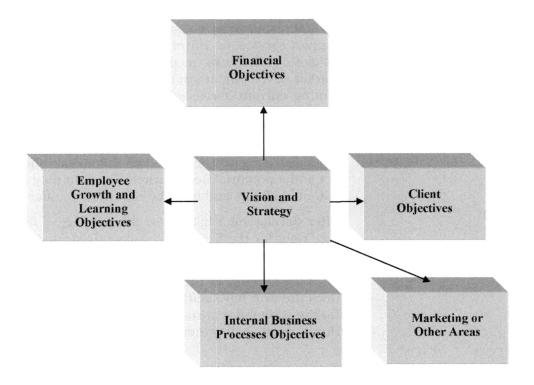

Financial Area

The financial area is one with which all accountants are familiar and have traditionally stressed. The firm's performance in terms of sustainable growth is perhaps the ultimate definition of success from a financial perspective. Financial results, however, tell the firm what *has* happened rather than what *will* happen. This is why the Balanced Scorecard approach requires the firm to consider other areas (clients, internal systems, and employee growth and learning).

Clients Area

Without satisfied and loyal clients, the firm will be unable to achieve its financial objectives of sustainable growth. "The customer perspective," according to Norton and Kaplan, "defines the value proposition for targeted customer segments."[4]

Internal Systems/Business Processes Area

The firm needs to determine which internal systems and business processes must be developed, improved, or modified to better serve internal and external clients. Such processes may include marketing, work flow, decision-making, internal and external communication, recruitment, orientation, performance management, and of course, compensation.

---

[4]Norton and Kaplan, p. 7.

Many of these systems are technology-based or, at a minimum, require technology support.

Employee Growth and Learning Area

Unless employees (including owners) develop technical, conceptual, and relationship competencies, it is difficult to elevate the level and depth of service to clients. The employee perspective describes how the people will be trained and organized to support the firm's strategy.

The following table captures how a firm's strategy and the four key areas flow into one another:

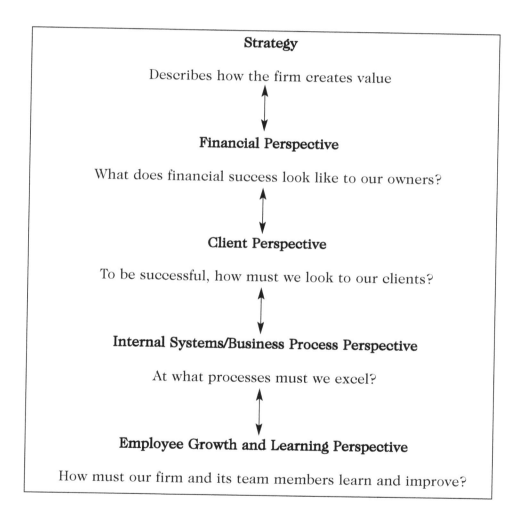

Strategy

Describes how the firm creates value

Financial Perspective

What does financial success look like to our owners?

Client Perspective

To be successful, how must we look to our clients?

Internal Systems/Business Process Perspective

At what processes must we excel?

Employee Growth and Learning Perspective

How must our firm and its team members learn and improve?

BUILDING THE SCORECARD

In Chapter 4, we discuss mission (why we exist), vision (what we want to become), and values (what behaviors are important to us). The Balanced Scorecard takes us one step further toward implementing the mission, with emphasis on strategy development and the use of strategy maps which visually translate the strategy.

The next step is for the firm or practice unit to develop the actual scorecard, which consists of a set of objectives, various types of measures, success targets for each measure, and specific action steps or tasks for each objective. A word of warning: Most firms initially try to capture too many measures. With four or more areas, you want no more than two or three measures per area. The following is a typical scorecard template.

Scorecard Template

Area	Objective	Measures (Lagging, Leading, and Real Time)	Target	Task(s)
Financial				
Clients				
Internal system/ business process				
Employee growth/learning				
(For additional areas)				

Objectives

Objectives tell you what you must do to execute your strategy. Paul Niven, in *Balanced Scorecard Step-by-Step: Maximizing Performance and Maintaining Results*, notes, "The best way to create performance objectives is to examine each perspective [area] of the Balanced Scorecard in the form of a question."[5]

- What financial steps are necessary to ensure the execution of our strategy?
- Who are our targeted customers and what is our value proposition in serving them?
- To satisfy our customers and shareholders, at what processes must we excel?
- What capabilities and tools do our employees require to help them execute our strategy?[6]

Performance Measures

Performance measures, as Paul Niven describes, are used to determine whether the firm is meeting its objectives and moving toward successful implementation of its strategy.[7] This section discusses performance measure types and performance measure selection, including the appropriate number of measures.

---

[5]Paul R. Niven, *Balanced Scorecard Step-by-Step: Maximizing Performance and Maintaining Results* (Hoboken, N.J.: John Wiley & Sons, 2002), p. 107.
[6]Niven, pp 107-8.
[7]Niven, p. 114.

Types of Performance Measure

There are three types of measures firms can select: lagging, leading, and real time. A lagging measure depicts the results of previous efforts. Traditionally, accountants have relied on lagging measures that are usually financial measures, such as revenue, net income per owner (NIPO), margins, realization, and utilization. These measures, however, don't tell you what to do to improve financial results. They only tell you what happened. Most financial measures are lagging measures. Last month revenues were "X," expenses were "Y," and profit or loss was "Z."

A leading measure, which is generally behavioral, predicts what might happen in the future. For example, you may track the number of sales appointments you attend each month. Let's say there are five in the first month, five more in the second month, and eight in the third month. Let's also say your goal was four per month. Such a measure tells you that revenues over the next several months could increase, provided these were qualified prospects and your professionals know how to develop and close. Leading measures are often called performance drivers. Unlike lagging measures, leading measures are often behavioral and useful in telling you how well you will likely do in the future.

A real-time measure tells you what is happening right now. Think about the gas gauge in your car. It tells you in real time how much gas you have left. At the same time, the speedometer tells you how fast the car is going. While real-time measures in an accounting firm may be more difficult to capture, they are still important. Employees could enter their time every hour. The internal accounting department could post cash throughout the day. The firm could track daily the number of hours spent face-to-face with a client or track weekly the number of proposals delivered.

For accounting firms, it may be best to focus on lagging and leading indicators. Imagine for a moment that you focus only on lagging measures. What real control or impact would you have on performance? Now imagine that you focus on leading measures, as well, such as:

- Building new niche areas.
- Creating new services.
- Prospecting specific clients.
- Making new business presentations.
- Asking for referrals from your key clients.
- Prospecting for leads and appointments during client seminars and conferences and symposia.
- Reducing work in progress.

If the number of new leads per month (a lagging measure) declines, you could increase your business development activities (leading measure). If the number of referrals from lawyers or bankers (a lagging measure) falls, you could increase the amount of time you spend with them or educate them more completely about what a good referral looks like (leading measure). Now *that* is proactive management!

Selecting Performance Measures

Every firm needs to identify what performance measures to track to achieve its desired objectives. This is not a "boilerplate" exercise. Selecting the right performance measures is critical in helping management make better decisions and motivating team members to behave in ways that support the firm's objectives. Choosing the right performance measures helps firms gain a competitive edge, both now and into the future.

The following guidelines may help you select the appropriate performance measures for your firm:

- Measures must tie into the firm's strategies. If, for example, the firm wants to be profitable the first year of its entry into the biotech market, one of the performance measures could be profitability per new engagement. If the objective is to build market share and not worry about current year profitability, the measure may be the number of new clients acquired.
- Measures should tie into owner and employee performance. For example, an owner who focuses on business development supports the firm's goal of bringing in new business. A possible measure could be the number of qualified appointments he or she is able to set. A tax preparer's measure could deal with the amount of time he or she takes to complete returns and whether the returns are completed by the agreed-upon deadlines. For staff accountants or new associates, it could be the number of times a project needs rework.
- While setting measures is necessary, team members and owners need to understand the strategy and measures, and buy into their importance. If they are unclear about what they are asked to accomplish, all the knowledge and skill in the world doesn't matter. They must understand how and why to apply them in their everyday activities.
- Finally, the measures need to be useful to management. Leading indicators cannot be faulty. Let's say you attempt to measure client satisfaction based on the number of complaints you receive from clients. Anecdotal evidence tells you, however, that clients don't complain, they just walk away. In this case, you have selected a faulty measure. (See Chapter 10 for a comprehensive list of measures.)

Number of Performance Measures

Most firms that undertake the Balanced Scorecard start with too many measures. We hear this from firms with revenue of less than $5 million and from firms with revenue of more than $100 million.

Considering that you may have four or five interrelated areas in which to develop measures, we believe you should have no more than two or three measures for each area. Tracking too many measures will surely cause you and your fellow owners to lose focus on what's truly important. A lot of money can be spent developing a tracking system with little return. It's best to go slowly until you understand what it takes to track your measures. Too much of a good thing, or in this case too many measures, is not healthy or wise.

Targets

According to Paul Niven, "A target can be defined as a quantitative representation of the performance measure at some point in the future (i.e., our desired future level of performance)."[8]

While there are financial benchmarks for the accounting and legal professions (examples include the Annual PCPS/Texas State Society Survey, the Rosenberg Survey, Inside Public Accounting's Annual Accounting Survey, and Of Counsel Annual Survey), firms need to determine their own targets or points of arrival (POA). Determining targets is nothing new for professional services firms. Firms generally set annual financial goals, set targets for accounts receivable days outstanding and work in progress, and assign billable hour targets for professionals and paraprofessionals. Firms have not been as diligent in setting goals in the other three areas of the Balanced Scorecard.

Without targets, firm management will never know how well it's achieving its objectives or implementing its strategies. Targets can be set for a month, quarter, year, or longer. Recall President Kennedy's 1961 target to put a man on the moon by the end of the decade. Whether your targets are long-term, mid-term, or short-term, they need to be specific. And while targets can be determined by senior management, you will get more buy-in if they are determined by the practice areas, niche groups, and others with final approval from senior management.

Tasks or Action Steps

After determining goals, measures, and targets, the final step is to develop specific action steps or tasks. These identify who will do what by when.

Sample Balanced Scorecard Templates

The following table shows a completed template for employee progress. The objective is to develop team member and owner marketing skills. The leading measures are the number of team members and owners who attend training and acquire marketing skills. The lagging measure is the amount of new billings as a result of developing the skills. Our example includes three targets that measure success. The first is having 80 percent of staff and owners trained by 2008. The second is having 100 percent trained by 2009. The third is $10,000 in billings for each individual who completed the training.

---

[8]Niven, p. 181.

Employee Growth and Learning

Area	Objective	Measure(s) (Lagging, Leading, And Real Time)	Target	Tasks
Employee Growth and Learning	Develop employee and owner marketing skills	1. Number of staff trained by 2008 2. Number of owners trained by 2009 3. Amount of new business developed by each attendee	1. 80% of staff acquire skills by 2008 2. 100% of owners acquire skills by 2009 3. $10,000 of new billings	Tom to contract with outside sales training professionals who design a program that exactly meets our needs by June 30.

STRATEGY MAPS

Recall that a strategy is an assumption of what may happen if everything goes right. If I do "A" and the result is "B," then I should expect "C" to happen. The Balanced Scorecard requires firms to develop more than a list of independent objectives. It requires firms to determine how the various objectives in each of the key areas interrelate. In other words, how are the objectives interdependent? How do one area's objectives affect and support another area's objectives?

For example, you cannot expect to enter a new market unless your firm's employees develop better knowledge about how to attract and serve its clients. Your owners and employees won't spend "quality" time with clients unless they know what quality time is. They won't deliver timely services until you have processes in place that reduce redundancies and other inefficient activities. They won't likely bring in new business unless they have business development and listening skills and are measured and compensated for doing so.

We call this the "gas pedal/brake pedal" theory. As much as you apply your collective feet to the gas pedals (for example, strategies for attracting new clients, spending quality time with clients, timely services, and new business development), there are always brake pedals pushing back just as hard. As we mentioned previously, these brake pedals usually come in the form of people not knowing what to do, how to do it, or why to do it. This compels you to change the systems (for example, recruitment and selection, orientation, training and development, mentoring and coaching, performance management, and compensation) that either cause or allow these brake pedals.

Here's another example. Assume under the "Client" area in the "Employee Growth and Learning" table your objective is to "establish long-term client relationships." Your measures are (1) the amount of quality time (nonbillable) spent with key clients to understand their business and needs, and (2) key client retention rates. A target for quality time spent with clients could be 16 hours per year with key clients. The target for key client retention rate might be 98 percent.

There is one more thing you need to do. In addition to setting an objective of establishing long-term client relationships, you must consider what else needs to be done to make that objective a reality. From an internal processing perspective you will need some sort of client relationship management (CRM) system to support your efforts. It could be as simple as a three-ring binder, an Excel spreadsheet, Microsoft Outlook, Goldmine, or a more sophisticated CRM (client relationship management) program. If you don't have a system in place, you won't be able to keep track of client contact and the nature of your discussions, methodology for follow-up, and ultimate outcomes.

In addition, your owners and team members are not likely to spend time with clients and talk about their business needs unless you help them develop specific competencies so they can prepare for, structure, and follow up these meetings. We trust you see how these areas are becoming interrelated and how a strategy map helps you visualize the interdependence of objectives.

Kaplan and Norton describe four ways in which creating value from intangible assets is different from creating value by managing tangible and financial assets.

1. Value creation is indirect. Intangible assets, such as competencies, training, and knowledge, usually don't have a direct effect on the financial outcome of a firm. Rather, there is a cause and effect relationship. As employees and owners become more highly skilled, they provide higher value services to clients, which in turn generate higher fees and better profits for the firm.

2. Value is contextual. "The value," according to Kaplan and Norton, "of an intangible asset depends on its alignment with the strategy." If your firm's strategy is to grow, but your training does not provide the necessary skills in business development, it won't have as much value for the firm as a training program that provides the firm with these skills. If your strategy is to grow, but owners and employees are not compensated for engaging in business development, little value can be created—even though they may have business development skills.

3. Value is potential. Kaplan and Norton note that, "The cost of investing in an intangible asset represents a poor estimate of its value to the organization." We cannot tell you how many firm leaders we have talked with who do not understand this point. What is the potential value of a lateral hire with specialized knowledge in one of your niches? What is the potential value of an internal process that tracks client satisfaction and loyalty on a real time basis?

4. Assets are bundled. An accounting firm's biggest asset is its people. If your people are not aligned behind the firm's mission and vision (see Chapter 3), maximum value will not be created. Individual owners and employees bring more value to an organization when they work together interdependently rather than when they work in isolation or independently.

The strategy map that follows is for a mid-sized accounting firm and shows how strategy links the intangible assets to value-creating processes. We have found firms as small as $3 million using strategy maps, and we consistently help firms, regardless of size, create them.

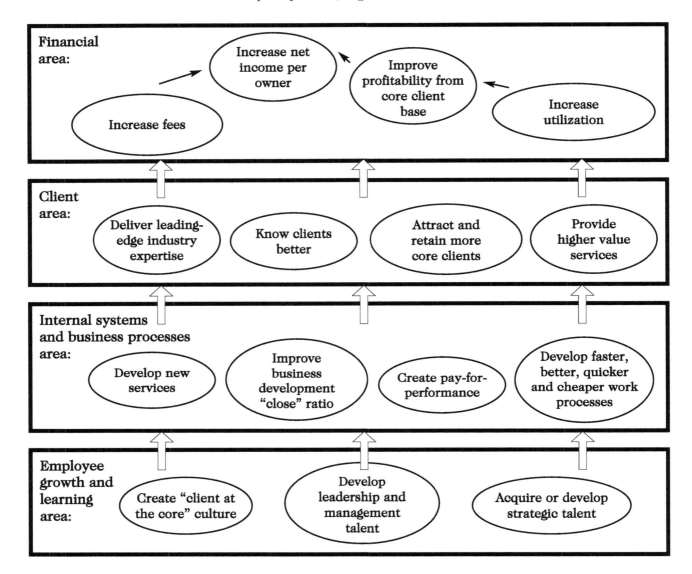

FINAL THOUGHTS

While the Balanced Scorecard process focuses on key measures necessary to achieve stated objectives, the process is really more about strategy implementation. It's only by focusing on measures and targets that a firm can determine how well its strategy is working, how effective its processes are, and how well people are producing.

When applied properly in professional services firms, the Balanced Scorecard creates the following organizational benefits:

■ Defines specific objectives for both the firm and for each aspect of its practice units

- Builds consensus on what should be measured at the firm, department, niche, engagement, or individual level
- Identifies targets or successes at each stage of the process (milestones)
- Shows how different objectives interrelate through the use of strategy maps
- Defines the process for successfully meeting objectives
- Improves internal communications among the owners and between owners and employees
- Places emphasis on both financial and non-financial (client, employee growth and learning, and internal systems and business processes) measures
- Produces greater owner and employee accountability
- Generates superior financial results for shareholders

To keep the Balanced Scorecard from becoming overwhelming, we suggest you start with only a few measures you can track without fail. Based on your experience, you can then expand the process and create separate scorecards for each department, niche, and service area.

6

COMPENSATION TERMINOLOGY AND CRITERIA

"The beginning of wisdom is the definition of terms."

—Plato

Based on Plato's quote, it seems appropriate to begin our discussion of compensation systems by explaining general terms common to compensation systems. This chapter discusses not only compensation terms, but also the criteria many firms currently use for evaluating performance.

COMPENSATION TERMINOLOGY

In this section, we define and discuss four key components of owner compensation: base pay, return on capital, bonus, and return on equity. We also explore the concepts of total compensation.

Base Pay

Base pay can best be defined as the pay for a job or position excluding additional payments or allowances. The difficult questions include:

- What is the base value of any given position?
- How much should you pay?
- How do you determine what the pay should be?

These are merely some of the questions owners of public accounting firms and human resources professionals ask themselves consistently when hiring new employees or admitting new owners.

For most workers (with the exception of C-level executives such as CEOs, CFOs, and CIOs), base pay is the essence of their compensation. This is historically true for owners of public accounting firms. As we look at a typical accounting firm, base pay is often determined by position. For each position in the firm (for example, staff accountant, senior, supervisor, manager, and director), firms generally create a base-pay range that is often determined by market pressures, applicants' years of experience or negotiation skills, and a list of other criteria that may or may not have anything to do with what it takes to get the job done.

Profession Averages

Exhibit 6–1, "Robert Half 2006 Public Accounting Salary Statistics," outlines selected statistics from the Robert Half 2006 Salary Guide. According to this guide, public accounting salaries ranged from $42,750 to $60,000 (large firms), to $36,750 to $46,000 (medium firms), to $35,500 to $42,500 (small firms) for individuals with 1 to 3 years of experience. Individuals with a master's degree or CPA certification earned up to 10 percent more.

Starting salaries for owners in public accounting firms averaged around $175,000 and rise well into the six-figure and even seven-figure range depending on experience, size of the firm, and overall profitability. Directors can expect salaries of $85,500 to $130,000 (large firms), $76,750 to $111,000 (medium firms), and $71,500 to $90,250 (small firms). Managers can earn salaries of $70,250 to $95,000 (large firms), $66,500 to $83,250 (medium firms), and $60,000 to $72,500 (small firms).

Importance of Base Pay

Base pay is especially critical among owners in a firm because it sets up a formal or informal pecking order. An individual's base pay often signifies his or her value to the organization. Most owners refer to their base pay as a draw or salary. We find owners tend to pay more attention to what they get paid in comparison to another owner (relative pay) than to the actual dollars they receive (actual pay). We have witnessed countless cases in which Owner A is upset because Owner B is paid $3,000 more when, in fact, each owner is paid well over $300,000.

Base pay for most accountants is the largest portion of total compensation. This is a fundamental cause of a number of compensation issues faced by accounting firms today. A disproportional percentage of base pay tends to create a system of entitlement and makes change harder to implement.

In *Paying for Performance*, Peter T. Chingos points out several instances in which base pay may become too cumbersome for proper performance and rewards, including:[1]

- Too much focus on base pay as the primary element of compensation
- Too much effort on cheating the system
- Too little education on what is required for performance increases
- Too little emphasis on contingent compensation as a motivator

Ed McGaughey, Director, KPMG's Performance & Compensation Consulting Practice notes that "basing pay on wage trends or cost of

---

[1]Peter T. Chingos, *Paying for Performance: A Guide to Compensation Management*, 2d ed. Hoboken, N.J.: John Wiley and Sons, 2002.

living, as opposed to value creation, will most often limit accomplishment of strategic pay objectives."[2]

Current Methods for Calculating Owner Base Pay

Not too long ago, we asked a handful of managing owners the following three questions:

1. Do you have a minimum level of compensation for a new owner? If so, how is it determined?
2. Do you determine the market value (street value) of your owners?
3. How do you determine new owner compensation (for example, formula and gut feeling)?

While this was not a statistically valid survey, it does give a flavor of what firms are currently doing. Here are some of the replies.

"Our first-year owners start at $131,000 (and the base gets adjusted each year for inflation), and merged or acquired owners come in at a rate similar to what they were making. Our draws get increased (for inflation) each year for the first eight years until the base draw is $210,000. Our target for base draw as a percentage of total owner comp (firm-wide average rather than by individual) is a maximum of 50 percent. This year, we are at 49 percent."

"At this time, we do not have a formalized minimum level of compensation. I would say that, informally, we have used the $125,000 range."

"We determine the initial compensation based on the following relationships: (1) billable hours, book of business, or technical specialties; and, (2) if it is a lateral move, we add 'what it would take to get him or her to join the firm.'"

"If someone is coming up internally, I would look at the spread of what they were making as base pay as a manager to their base pay as an owner to make sure it is worthwhile. My recent base was $125,000. If an owner is coming in via a merger or acquisition, I would make sure the total package is more than what they were receiving previously."

"We have never considered 'street value' of an owner, but we do keep an eye on the various firm surveys to ensure our owners are compensated similarly to firms of our size in markets that are similar to ours."

"We are moving in that direction [that is, toward street value]."

"On an annual basis, I look to see if base pay should be increased, based on both public and private pay benchmarks."

Even though the above was not meant to be a scientific study of determining base pay for owners, it does suggest that many firms have no objective or systematic approach for determining base pay.

---

[2]Chingos, p. 8.

An Objective Approach to Base Pay

Nicholas J. Mastracchio, in *Mergers and Acquisitions of CPA Firms: A Guide to Practice Valuation*, provides a formula to determine the fair value of an owner's services.[3] Mastracchio's assertion is that the money owners take out of the firm is a combination of both a fair compensation and a return on their ownership investment. He believes that if the firm (1) has a simple or complex compensation formula for owners that identifies and values key criteria (for example, billable hours, new business, and client service), (2) quantifies each criterion as salary before equity distribution, and (3) has a process and results that are reasonable, then fair compensation has been identified.

One could definitely argue about the reasonableness of many compensation processes. For those firms that do not use the above approach or do not know what fair salaries should be and do not want to estimate them, Mastracchio provides the following formula that can, at least, serve as a starting point for further discussion about fair salaries for owners.[4]

His formula is based on the salaries of others in the firm, mainly managers and directors. Staff salaries (A) are to staff billing rates (B) as owner salaries (C) are to owner billing rates (D). Think of the following equation:

$$\frac{A \text{ (Staff Salaries)}}{B \text{ (Staff Billing Rates)}} = \frac{C \text{ (Owner Salaries)}}{D \text{ (Owner Billing Rates)}}$$

The calculation is based upon a ratio of known facts. Firms have information about A, B, and D. Having this information, they can then solve for C (owner salaries) as follows:

(Staff Salaries × Owner Billing Rates)/Staff Billing Rates = Owner Salaries

For large firms, Mastracchio suggests using manager and senior salaries, and for small firms, he believes full-time professional staff salaries can be used.

Consider a hypothetical large firm. If the average salary for managers is $85,000, average manager billing rates are $143. This assumes the firm calculates billing rates by dividing the employee's fully loaded cost by 2,080 hours and then multiplying that amount by 3.5 (assuming $85,000/2080 times 3.5 multiple). By assuming that the average owner billing rates are $225, owner salaries would be calculated as follows:

($85,000 × $225)/$143 = $133,741

Under this hypothetical example, $133,741 is a fair base compensation for an owner in the firm. Any amounts paid over $133,741 would be considered a bonus or a return on ownership interest. While this method is not without issues, it can provide a starting point for determining a fair base compensation for owners.

---

[3]Nicholas J. Mastracchio, *Mergers and Acquisitions of CPA Firms: A Guide to Practice Valuation.* New York: American Institute of Certified Public Accountants, 1998.
[4]Mastracchio, p. 103.

Return on Capital

If a firm requires its owners to make a capital contribution, the firm usually pays interest on the owner's accrual capital account. Some firms pay a fixed percentage while others pay from one to three percentage points over prime. This portion of an owner's compensation is usually paid monthly to the owner and is paid before any bonuses or return on equity.

Owners are making greater investments in technology, real estate, and marketing than ever before. It may seem that new owners and even existing owners only want to take money out of the firm. They often find it hard to think of a practice like a real business in which assets are bought, people are paid salaries, and investments are made for the future. So, a few years ago, we asked several well-known consultants such questions as, How much accrual basis capital should a firm maintain? What are you seeing in the market today? How are firms determining capital accounts? What's the rationale behind their methods, and how are owners coping with keeping more money in their firms?[5]

Don Scholl responded, "No matter if the firm is a sole practitioner or multioffice, multiowner entity, each firm should require some capital to fund its working capital needs and any capital requirements for equipment and property. I have always felt that, at a minimum, capital accounts should be 20 percent of a firm's budgeted collections. This minimum anticipates that the firm will be using its line of credit for some part of the year. Further, there is a positive element about having a low capital requirement. It can force the owners to become aggressive in collecting accounts receivable."

Marc Rosenberg felt that "sophisticated firms will set a target for capital. The most common target is a percentage of net fees, usually 20 percent to 30 percent. But the vast majority of firms are not this formal and do not set any target for capital. Capital is as it is. The key, from a cash flow or capital-planning standpoint, is to avoid paying compensation to owners before WIP and A/R is collected."

Chris Frederiksen added, "I've seen a few firms go as high as 50 percent of fees. But that is surely not the norm. In any case, the capital should at least equal the net income of the firm before any owner compensation. With regard to Don Scholl's comment, I would recommend to a million-dollar firm with net income of $350,000 to have at least that $350,000 in capital."

Bonus

Bonuses are normally paid to owners after the return on capital has been paid. Bonuses can range from 10 percent of base compensation to more than 100 percent. We are familiar with firms in which owners can receive from two to three times their base as a year-end bonus.

For bonuses to be effective, we suggest they be substantial. An owner whose base compensation is $300,000 may not be motivated to make

---

[5]"The Role of Ownership: A Roundtable Discussion," Partner Advantage Advisory, vol. 2 (2004): 1-6.

significant effort during the year for a $20,000 or $30,000 bonus because it does not significantly change his or her lifestyle. We believe bonuses should be at least 20 percent or more of the base compensation to be meaningful.

The basic purpose of a bonus is to reward performance beyond expectations. In our minds, extraordinary performance means doing something beyond what is expected. It's like hitting a grand slam. If owners must debate whether performance was extraordinary or not, it probably wasn't.

Another purpose of a bonus is to reward extraordinary performance for both owners and employees without increasing base compensation and thus facing the possibility of paying for mediocre performance in subsequent years. We believe it is better economically for a firm to provide bonuses to employees rather than inflate base salaries needlessly.

Return on Equity

In many firms, there is no relationship between an individual's capital account and his or her equity in the firm. Some firms have a minimum capital contribution requirement, and equity is merely allocated to new owners.

Equity payments are often considered as entitlement payments because they have nothing to do with current performance. Only 28 of the 423 (or 6.6 percent) firms that responded to the 2006 Compensation Survey use a pure ownership percentage method as their owner compensation system. All 28 of these firms except 1 are under $5 million in net fees. The exception is between $5 million and $10 million. Of respondents who use the ownership percentage method, 67 percent believe the system is designed not to be fair or to be only somewhat fair.

The reason for the lack of fairness is obvious. Owners with larger equity percentages reap the benefits from other owners who may be doing more work and bringing in more new business. Only a strong-willed managing owner with high equity can keep this system alive. The other owners in these firms often operate as senior managers and are given little opportunity to provide input into the management or direction of the firm.

There should, of course, be some return for ownership as a percentage of total compensation. While it currently varies from firm to firm, we believe it should generally be between 15 percent and 20 percent. If the firm pays an ownership dividend, it should be paid after owner draws, bonuses, and returns on capital have been paid.

As our 2006 Compensation Survey showed, most firms today realize there is little, if any, correlation between equity and compensation. There are two times when equity does become important. First, when the firm is sold and owners distribute the proceeds of the sale. Second, when an owner retires and the retirement formula is based on the equity percentage.

When we asked members of the New Horizon Group about how a firm decides how much ownership (equity percentage) to assign to a new owner, we received an array of answers.

For example, Marc Rosenberg responded that "this is one of the most comical and haphazard areas of CPA firm practice management. Most firms, if they were honest, would admit that there has been no coherent or consistent system used to determine ownership percentage. This is a big mistake because if ownership is used in important ways, like allocating income or determining retirement benefits, it will make the owners very unhappy when the inevitable arises (an owner with a high ownership percentage is awarded compensation or retirement benefits that are far in excess of what he deserves)."

Bob Martin cautioned everyone "to remember that ownership percentage has an impact on owners in five possible ways: (1) voting, (2) compensation, (3) retirement benefits, (4) determining buy-in amount, and (5) allocating assets and liabilities from the sale or liquidation of the firm. But the impact and influence of ownership percentage can be eliminated in all but number 5."

Steve Erickson thought that "the larger the role that ownership plays on the above, the more problems and complications you will have. Conversely, if you minimize the role of ownership percentage, it makes it easier to bring in new owners and deal with each of the above areas separately."

And Rita Keller felt that "when it comes to compensation, it should be allocated primarily on the basis of performance, not ownership. However, there are still a lot of small firms paying senior owners on ownership."

Don Scholl had a different take on the question: "Buy-in should be determined not by ownership percentage but by what the current owners feel is a meaningful number they want each new owner to contribute. For example, take the case of a four-owner, $3 million firm with capital of $1 million. If you admit a fifth owner and want that person to be a 5 percent owner, that would result in a buy-in amount of $200,000, which today is considered by most firms to be higher than what young people are willing to pay. The firm is better off deciding on a meaningful amount, say $50,000, and working backward to decide on the ownership percentage. In this case, the new owner would own 1.2 percent of the firm [50,000 divided by 4,050,000]."[6]

TOTAL COMPENSATION

Total compensation is a concept used to encompass the entire range of wages and benefits, both current and deferred, that owners and employees receive. Total compensation includes all types of employee compensation combined: wages and salary, bonuses, nonwage cash payments, and benefits. For an owner, this includes draw and salary, bonuses, return on capital, return on equity, any matching contributions to a 401(k), deferred compensation, and firm payments toward health care, life/disability insurance, and other benefits.

Total compensation is important in any organization because most employees and many owners do not understand total compensation costs. Consider the following items that often go unnoticed and unappreciated by employees: (1) training costs, (2) advanced-degree tuition

---

[6]"The Role of Ownership: A Roundtable Discussion," pp. 4-5.

reimbursement, and (3) additional time off. The true cost of your total compensation may be even more than you believe it is. This is why firms need to improve communication with employees about the total compensation they receive—not just salaries, wages, bonuses and other obvious benefits.

At the 2004 Workforce Planning and Development Conference, Elliot R. Sussesles, senior vice president of the Segal Company, provided the following information when discussing whether a firm's total compensation structure supports employees' perceptions and values:

- Employees with a working spouse may view health insurance as less valuable than pay increases or other benefits.
- Employees without children may see little value in child-related benefits (dependent coverage, 529 plans, or orthodontia plan).
- Employees in single-income households may view job security as more important than pay or benefits.
- Employees age 45 and older are usually more focused on retirement benefits than are younger employees.

Our best advice is to review your current range of benefits and the flexibility that employees have in selecting them. Once this is done, we recommend that you create a short document that outlines the firm's compensation philosophy and guiding principles.

Most major corporations, universities, and other entities share such documents with everyone in the organization, and they provide clarity about the firm's compensation program and principles. Exhibit 6–2, "Sample Firm Compensation Philosophy and Guiding Principles," provides an example of one such document.

COMPENSATION CRITERIA

In successful compensation systems, owners know what counts and what does not—with no second guessing.

We selected 18 criteria for our 2006 Compensation Survey and asked firms to identify whether they use each criterion and how important each is (from very unimportant and somewhat unimportant to somewhat important and very important). The results are summarized in Exhibit 6–3, "Compensation Criteria." Listed below are the top five criteria firms identified as "very important" in determining compensation.

- Book of business   26%
- Fees collected   25%
- Personal billable hours   18%
- New business development   17%
- Ownership percentage   17%

Even as we realize there can be many different ways to interpret the following, we believe it is helpful to define and discuss each of these criteria. The 18 criteria are listed in the following sections, with our descriptions.

Book of Business

Book of business was rated as the top compensation criteria in our survey. This is not surprising because business development is the lifeblood of any organization, including accounting firms! A book of business can best be defined as revenue for those clients that fall under an individual owner's billing run. In other words, these are the clients for which an owner has overall responsibility. They may not be the clients the owner actually brought in. In many firms, clients brought into the firm by its rainmakers are often transitioned immediately to more client-service-oriented owners.

The overall dollar amount of an owner's book of business is important because it is one clear measure of current potential contribution to the firm. The overall dollar amount of the book of business by itself, however, is not necessarily the best criterion for financial contribution to the firm, as we will discuss in the next section.

Client or Book Gross Profitability

We should note that more firms are looking at the profitability of an owner's book of business in addition to its overall dollar amount. If you analyze gross profitability at the client or book of business level, you may be surprised by your findings. One firm that performed this analysis found that 85 percent of its gross margin came from only 50 of its top clients.

The process is simple. Take a 12-month period (usually a calendar year). For each client, determine the amount of cash that was received and the amount of time (at cost) that was spent on the client. Include owner time in your calculation. This gives you a gross profit figure. To determine net profit, you can simply allocate a general overhead expense to each client.

When considering an owner's book of business, it is important to understand the following:

- Which owner has the most profitable book of business
- Which clients are the most profitable for the firm
- Which clients lose money for the firm

This can be used not only for compensation purposes, but also for culling the client base in instances where there is more work to do than available time or personnel.

Cross-Selling

Anecdotal evidence suggests that the more services a client uses, the less likely the client is to disengage the firm. Banks discovered this many years ago and do a good job of securing a customer's checking account, home mortgage, certificates of deposit, and the like. To determine which clients are using multiple services, you can create a simple client matrix within Microsoft Excel that lists client names in Column A and firm services in Row 1. Then, you can simply place an "X" in the appropriate cells.

Fees Collected

Fees collected ranked second in our list of 18 criteria. This is an easy measure to track and is more meaningful than chargeable or billable hours. Fees collected can also be linked to client satisfaction with work product and timeliness of delivery. Clients who are satisfied are more likely to pay quickly and have fewer write-downs and write-offs.

Firm Management

Corporate America recognizes, perhaps to a fault, the value of management. Most CEOs in the corporate world are highly compensated. According to Lawrence Mishel at the Economic Policy Institute, "In 2005, an average CEO was paid 821 times as much as a minimum wage earner." Last year, according to the Economic Policy Institute, the average CEO was paid $10.9 million a year, or 262 times an average worker's earnings of $41,861. Now, we do not expect such a gap will soon become prevalent in CPA firms, but it does show the importance of management's role in any business.

According to John P. Weil & Company, some professional services firms do not recognize the contribution of effective firm management to the firm's overall success (or lack thereof). In many firms, management is not a factor in compensation. Any organization unwilling to pay for proper management, however, will have little long-term, effective leadership. Effective management, therefore, should be recognized and compensated.

The accounting profession has begun to recognize the need for firm management and leadership. The primary leadership roles in a public accounting firm generally include the managing owner, the executive committee, and department heads (such as audit, tax, and consulting). Their responsibilities include setting the vision and strategic direction, building long-term value, identifying potential new opportunities, engaging in practice development, and creating owner alignment. People in management positions should have a significant portion of their compensation based on firm goal achievement rather than personal goals. By doing this, the firm sends a message to owners that management responsibilities have similar importance as billable hours or client work. Billable hours pay us today while effective firm leadership and management pay us in the future.

Industry Experience and Expertise

As firms begin to specialize, owners who have industry or niche expertise add more value to the firm's value proposition. There is a wide gap between the tax owner who is a generalist and the tax owner who is an expert in estate planning issues for family-owned and closely held businesses. The first owner is competing against every tax practitioner in the market, while the second has unique and specialized consulting skills that may provide clients with exceptional value-added advice and service. Owners who have experience in and deep knowledge of an industry are usually more valuable to the firm and its clients than the generalist owner.

Managed Charged Hours

Building and managing a book of business is critical to a firm's current well being and long-term success. It may, over the long run, be even more important than bringing in new business. Let us explain.

Owner A is the classic rainmaker. She loves bringing in business and then going on to the next exciting opportunity. The firm has been impressed with Owner A's ability to bring in new clients but has never analyzed how profitable these clients actually are.

Owner B is the classic minder. He does not bring in a lot of new clients but is outstanding at expanding business to his current client base. This work is less costly to acquire and keeps other owners and employees busy throughout the year. Let's also assume this work is more profitable.

Both owners help the firm grow. Over the long run, Owner B's contribution to net income per owner may be significantly more than Owner A's.

Owners who increase the hours they manage, either by cross-selling or expanding services to existing clients, should be recognized for doing so. Their work, while often considered less glamorous than rainmaking, is an extremely valuable contribution to the firm. If the firm is unable to nurture and sustain its current client relationships, the job of the rainmaker would be much more difficult.

Mentoring and Training Employees

Those who develop technically competent employees, solid professionals, and future leaders must also be rewarded. Owners who take time and make an effort to mentor, train, and develop others (or develop the systems that support such efforts) must surely be rewarded for activities that build future capacity.

New Business Development

New business is the lifeblood of any organization and keeps a firm vibrant by providing employees opportunities with new and varied types of engagements. Imagine a firm with client attrition that averages 10 percent per year. Assuming this is true, the firm could not exist for long without new clients and new work.

New business development or origination is often recognized by firms as one of the top evaluation and compensation criteria. During the last several years, firms have also started to pay more attention to the profitability of new business as well as top-line revenue. Beyond the above, many firms are striving much harder to ensure that new clients fit an ideal client profile, and as a result, have developed reasonably detailed client acceptance procedures.

Many people believe new business development is an art, but it is also a "science"—a skill that can be learned. There are a number of good business development training programs available to accountants, and The Growth Partnership offers a workshop titled "The Reluctant Salesperson: *A Realistic Approach to Practice Development for the CPA*™."

Ownership Percentage

Equity owners provide working capital, meet payroll, sign real estate leases, and maintain overall responsibility for firm liability. They should, therefore, be given a certain return for the risks they take. In smaller and younger firms, the founders are indeed entrepreneurs. In larger firms and those that have transitioned successfully from the first generation of owners to the second, the owners are generally less entrepreneurial because they have inherited a well-established business.

The return to which equity owners are entitled for their investment and risk is, of course, open to great debate.

Personal Productivity (Billable Hours and Charge Hours)

Personal productivity is generally evaluated either by the number of charge hours (work in progress) or by the number of billable hours an owner produces. Billable hours are always more valuable than charge hours. Personal productivity, in our minds, is even more complex. Consider the following scenarios; which owner do you believe is more productive?

> *Owner A has 1,500 charge hours but abuses employees and requires hours of personal counseling by management. Owner B has 1,300 charge hours but trains and mentors employees consistently, participates enthusiastically in change efforts, and serves as a model owner.*

Measuring productivity is further complicated by the efficiency with which engagements are managed or the number of clients an owner serves.

Consider another scenario. Again, which owner would you consider to be more productive?

> *Owner X delegates work to other owners and employees in the firm (that is, leverages). Owner Y, all else being equal, hoards work for himself.*

While personal production should certainly be *a* factor, be sure you understand the real productivity behind (or in addition to) the numbers.

Professional and Community Involvement

Both professional and community involvement can enhance the firm's image, reputation, and prestige. Participation in professional activities (for example, speaking at an AICPA or state society conference) provides the firm exposure to other professionals. Speaking at, or participating in, civic, charitable, and niche or industry activities provides exposure to potential clients and referral sources. Through these networking activities, firms can also maintain good relations with other firms, identify and recruit future professionals, and serve as good citizens.

Participation in organizations can help an owner develop relationship-building and leadership skills. Personal stature in the community or profession adds to the stature of the firm, and an increase in stature or reputation is often a catalyst for attracting new clients.

Owners who engage in these activities should generally have the agreement of other owners in the firm that there is value in these activities (that is, there is some form of return on investment measurement).

Realization

Realization is the percentage of standard fees on a client engagement that is actually billed after any write-downs and write-ups. Standard (gross) fees are commonly referred to as total chargeable hours at standard billing rates. If Owner A has a billing rate of $225 per hour and spends 20 hours on a client project, the standard fees or gross fees for this project are $5,000. If Owner A decides to bill the client only $4,500, the realization is 90 percent ($4,500/$5,000). For whatever reason, Owner A decided he cannot bill the client more than $4,500. Some firms confuse realization with client profitability. There *is* a difference.

Seniority

"The older I get, the wiser I am." Well, that adage may be true—or not. Neither age nor seniority has anything to do with wisdom, and we know it has nothing to do with contributions to the firm. Yes, there are some senior owners who contribute more than anyone else in the firm, but there is no correlation between age or seniority and firm contribution.

In some firms, there is certainly a perceived value in tenure and seniority. Law firms that use a lockstep method of compensation and accounting firms that allocate profits based on points (which usually increase over the years) more heavily reward owners based on longevity.

However, the value of seniority can be difficult to define. Being with a firm for the most years does not necessarily mean an individual owner has the highest value. Rather, we believe the firm should look at the owner's contributions to the firm over the years:

- What has been the owner's contribution in terms of growth and name recognition?
- How has the owner spent his or her years developing new clients and maintaining existing ones?
- What has the owner done to enhance the firm's reputation?
- How has the owner helped develop and train younger staff members?

While owner tenure or seniority has had a strong influence on compensation in the past, most new compensation systems downplay this criterion or do not include it as a factor at all. Firms that favor tenure or seniority as a factor in compensation (a bonus distribution) generally have an owner group (or strong subset of senior owners) that may be uncomfortable with annual evaluations based on performance and are generally unable to grow at a fast pace.

Technical Expertise

In today's environment, technical expertise is a given; it is the "price of admission." But there are degrees of technical expertise. Is the tax owner with a master of science in taxation (MST) degree worth more than one without such advanced training? Is the owner who becomes the guru in estate tax worth more than the generalist who only completes Forms 1040? There is a real need to recognize such unique and specific competencies and what they mean to the firm's reputation, image, and economic results.

Specific technical expertise measures include, but may not be limited, to:

- *Know-what:* Degrees (for example, MBA or MST), licensures (for example, CPA or JD), certifications (for example, CVA, CFP, or DABFA), and other education that increases an individual's technical knowledge and equips him or her to provide a wide array of advice and counsel.
- *Know-how:* An individual with *know-how* can apply his or her *know-what* (often referred to as book knowledge) to real-life situations. For example, you can read about sailing all day long, understand all terms and nautical rules, but it is not until you get the boat in the water and begin to tack, come about, or jibe that you can move from *know-what* to *know-how*.
- *Know-why:* For long-term success, even *know-how* is not sufficient. Professionals need to move to the next level, *know-why*. This requires a professional to understand the interrelationship of the elements of a system. Individuals with a deep understanding of *know-why* can tell you the consequences of the actions that will likely happen when you change one element of a system long before the final report is presented. Think about the complexity of developing an estate plan and the knowledge required to make sure all pieces of the plan fit and work together.

Technical expertise can also be evaluated by observing and measuring the following owner talents:

- Creativity in problem solving
- Good oral and written communications
- Good on-the-spot judgment
- Good analytical skills
- Being able to handle complex problems
- Being able to meet deadlines

Utilization

Utilization is the amount of time employees and owners are chargeable. Rules of thumb are owners should be chargeable from 50 percent to 60 percent of the time, and employees should be chargeable approximately 70 percent of the time.

The calculation of utilization is quite simple. Divide an individual's chargeable hours by his or her total hours to determine the utilization percentage. For example, a person who charged 1,600 hours and worked

2,200 has a 72.7 percent utilization rate. You can also measure utilization on a departmental, team, industry, and firm basis.

Utilization was not one of the top five criteria. There is a fatal flaw in putting too much emphasis on this criterion because it uses chargeable time in the calculation. It is an easy criterion to manipulate. An owner merely needs to have a high level of chargeable time rather than billable time to make the utilization percentage look good. This is why firms place more emphasis on net fees collected than on utilization. As the saying goes, "cash is king."

Other Criteria

There are certainly other criteria firms use in determining owner compensation. Some firms evaluate an owner's compliance with the firm's policies. Other firms look at how well the owner gets along with other owners and employees. And still others consider the committees on which an owner has served during the year. Many owner behavioral criteria can often be captured by developing the firm's core values and measuring how well the owner lives them.

Criteria for Effective Compensation Systems

Exhibit 6–4, "Sample Indicators/Measures of Success," is a chart we often use in our compensation consulting. It provides a list of leading and lagging indicators that can be used in determining criteria for your compensation system. It is not meant to be all inclusive. We encourage you to look at it and add criteria that may better fit with your firm's culture.

We asked survey participants two follow-up questions. First, "How satisfied are you with the current criteria?" Second, "How satisfied do you believe your fellow owners are with the current criteria?"

Only 29 percent responded "very satisfied," and 44 percent said "somewhat satisfied" to the first question. For the second question, only 23 percent answered "very satisfied," but 50 percent replied "somewhat satisfied."

Finally, we asked survey participants to indicate which of the criteria *should* be used in their owner compensation system. Here are the top 10 responses ranked from highest to lowest:

1. Firm management — 82.8%
2. New business development (origination) — 73.4%
3. Fees collected — 65.8%
4. Book of business — 63.3%
5. Realization — 60.7%
6. Client or book gross profitability — 60.5%
7. Personal billable hours — 56.5%
8. Mentoring & training employees — 54.0%
9. Technical expertise — 49.2%
10. Community involvement — 41.5% ⎫ tied
10. Cross-selling — 41.5% ⎭

FINAL THOUGHTS

Before we end our discussion about criteria, we want to make one crucial claim. It is a mistake to hold all owners to the same criteria. Each owner in your firm has unique areas in which he or she generally excels. A good compensation system helps you to determine these areas, consider their relative importance, measure their impact, and reward the owner accordingly.

Each owner should be evaluated on each of the criteria based on his or her goals, role in the firm, and fit into the firm's overall strategy. For some, the highest level of technical competence is expected. For others, it could be mentoring. For others, client development.

Owner A is the great senior practice owner who needs to be good at a lot of things. He or she develops some business but has little firm management responsibilities. Owner B, on the other hand, is the rainmaker. He or she is expected to bring in a great deal of new business but does not manage client engagements or bill much. Owner C is the typical working owner. He or she is a strong technician and has little, if any, firm management responsibilities. The secret is to set expectations based on each owner's role and then compensate each owner based on how good he or she is in that role.

There are some criteria, however, to which all owners should be held and that should be applied equally, for example, living the firm's core values and following firm policies. At the end of the day, owners should be motivated to do what they like to do best, as long as it helps to achieve the level of excellence needed in today's competitive environment.

EXHIBIT 6–1   **Robert Half 2006 Public Accounting Salary Statistics**

Public Accounting—Audit, Tax, and Management Services (Large Firms) (a)

Experience/Title	2006 Salary Range
to 1 year (b)	$42,750–$52,000
1–3 years (b)	$48,750–$60,000
Senior (b)	$56,750–$75,000
Manager (b)	$70,250–$95,000
Manager/Director (b)	$85,500–$130,000

(a) $250+ million in sales

(b) add 10% for a graduate degree or CPA

Public Accounting—Audit, Tax, and Management Services (Medium Firms) (a)

Experience/Title	2006 Salary Range
to 1 year (b)	$36,750–$46,000
1–3 years (b)	$43,750–$53,000
Senior (b)	$50,000–$70,000
Manager (b)	$66,500–$83,250
Manager/Director (b)	$76,750–$111,000

(a) $25 to $250 million in sales

(b) add 10% for a graduate degree or CPA

Public Accounting—Audit, Tax, and Management Services (Small Firms) (a)

Experience/Title	2006 Salary Range
to 1 year (b)	$35,500–$42,500
1–3 years (b)	$39,500–$47,000
Senior (b)	$47,000–$59,250
Manager (b)	$60,000–$72,500
Manager/Director (b)	$71,500–$90,250

(a) up to $25 million in sales

(b) add 10% for a graduate degree or CPA

(Source: 2006 Robert Half and Accountemps Salary Guide)

EXHIBIT 6–2   **Sample Firm Compensation Philosophy and Guiding Principles**

Eagle & Rice Compensation Philosophy and Guiding Principles:

- To attract, retain, reward, and motivate the productivity and commitment of highly qualified employees and owners.
- To provide flexibility appropriate to the dynamic challenges facing professionals today.
- To help the firm compete successfully for employees with the mix of skills vital to its mission.
- To provide a flexible benefits package that allows employees to choose the appropriate benefits for their individual situation.
- To embrace a pay-for-performance system of total compensation
  —We reward outstanding performance.
  —Base compensation reflects above market average.
  —Bonuses reflect performance.
  —Primary responsibility for determining pay rests with you and your supervisor based on achieving goals set forth in your win-win agreement.
- Market considerations, overall firm profitability, or regulatory demands may cause the firm to change its compensation and benefits practices. Employees should be aware that their benefits may change from time to time as a result of firm policy decisions.

EXHIBIT 6–3   Compensation Criteria

	Currently Used	Not Currently Used	Very Unimportant	Somewhat Unimportant	Somewhat Important	Very Important
Book of business	44%	35%	4%	5%	24%	26%
Client or book gross profitability	23%	58%	2%	4%	21%	15%
Community involvement	19%	63%	4%	15%	20%	2%
Cross selling	15%	68%	4%	9%	19%	3%
Fees collected	37%	40%	4%	5%	24%	25%
Firm management	43%	32%	3%	9%	40%	13%
Industry experience/ expertise	13%	65%	3%	7%	26%	6%
Managed charged hours	30%	48%	3%	8%	28%	13%
Mentoring and training employees	20%	60%	2%	11%	24%	7%
New business development (origination)	40%	40%	1%	7%	23%	17%
Ownership percentage	40%	35%	9%	12%	23%	17%
Personal billable hours	36%	39%	3%	7%	31%	18%
Personal charge hours	32%	45%	5%	10%	26%	13%
Professional involvement	17%	60%	4%	15%	20%	4%
Realization	33%	44%	3%	8%	28%	16%
Seniority	21%	57%	8%	13%	20%	6%
Technical expertise	19%	58%	3%	8%	26%	10%
Utilization	13%	64%	5%	11%	19%	5%

(Source: 2006 Compensation Survey)

EXHIBIT 6–4   **Sample Indicators/Measures of Success**

Leading Indicators/Measures of Success	*Lagging Indicators/Measures of Success*
■ Attendance/participation in firm or outside activities	■ Rainmaking
■ Team player	⬛ Alone
■ Meets deadlines	⬛ Together
■ 360-degree employee evaluation (core values)	■ Total hours worked
■ Technical skill development	■ Billable hours
■ Credential/licensure	■ Total revenue
■ Coordinates or facilitates staff training	■ Realization
■ Performs strategic client reviews	⬛ Firm-wide
■ Attends client meetings	⬛ Office
■ Gives seminars/workshops	⬛ Engagement or project
■ Quality of work	■ Profitability
■ Client satisfaction	⬛ Firm
■ Client relationship mgmt	⬛ Office
■ Client retention	⬛ Engagement or project
■ Community service/memberships	■ Contribution margin
■ Manages others	■ WIP
■ Mentors/coaches others	■ A/R (aging)
■ Responds to RFPs	■ Cross-sold services
■ Helps develop internal systems	■ Number of services provided to a client
■ Spends significant time learning client needs	■ Net fees realized
	■ Net fees realized per person
	■ Income per shareholder

7

CURRENT COMPENSATION METHODS

"Money was never a big motivation for me, except as a way to keep score. The real excitement is playing the game."

—Donald Trump

"The Donald" perhaps understood the nature and culture of public accounting firms when he wrote the above. While money isn't the be all and end all, it certainly influences owner behavior.

In the beginning of time, two CPAs came together, decided to share profits, and began the never-ending evolution of owner compensation systems.

It goes without saying that many of the compensation systems we discuss in this chapter have served firms well over the years and have served as a catalyst for accomplishing firm goals. At the same time, however, they may have inadvertently served as roadblocks that prevent firms from reaching their full potential.

In our 2006 Compensation Survey, we identified 10 often-used compensation systems and asked respondents to identify their plan if it was not listed. Of the 423 respondents, 55 selected the "other" category, which demonstrates the great variety of compensation systems. The "other" category was the third most selected.

The following chart shows responses to our 2006 Compensation Survey, ranked from highest to lowest, to the question, "What type of owner compensation system does the firm currently use?"

Method	Response Percent	Response Total
Formula (firm uses algebraic formula to determine compensation)	17.7%	75
Equal pay	15.8%	67
Other (combinations of the other methods)	13%	55
Managing owner decides	12.5%	53
All owners decide	10.9%	46
Ownership percentage	6.6%	28
Pay for performance	5.4%	23
Eat what you kill	5.4%	23
Compensation committee	5.2%	22
Executive committee	5%	21
Paper and pencil	2.4%	10

Source: 2006 Compensation Survey

The chart below illustrates the compensation method used according to firm size.

Compensation Method	2–4 owners	5–9 owners	10–23 owners	>24 owners	Total responses
Equal pay	49	3	0	0	52
Formula method	43	17	6	0	66
Managing owner	26	6	1	0	33
Compensation committee	5	5	8	3	21
Executive committee	3	6	5	2	16
All owners	26	10	0	0	36
Pay for performance	9	4	4	3	20
Paper and pencil	5	2	1	0	8
Ownership % method	18	4	0	0	22
Eat what you kill	14	3	1	0	18
Other	24	10	4	2	40
Totals	222	70	30	10	332

Source: 2006 Compensation Survey

In this chapter, we discuss the strengths and weaknesses of each method and the type of firm most likely to use a specific compensation system, plus a method not covered in the survey, the lockstep method. We should note that, in each of these methods, there is probability that subjective factors enter into the process and that some firms use a combination of these methods.

FORMULA METHOD

According to our survey, the formula method is used by 75 of the 423 responding firms. It appears, therefore, this is the most popular method among accounting firms today. This is echoed by the *2005 Rosenberg Survey* presented in Exhibit 7–1, "Compensation Systems by Firm Size—Rosenberg," and a Gary Boomer study presented in Exhibit 7–2, "Compensation Systems by Firm Size—Boomer." According to these surveys, the formula method is most popular with firms with more than two owners.

The formula method may also be the most popular with accountants because it relates best to the typical accountant personality. Accountants like numbers, and how can anyone argue with a formula? We learned in high school algebra how to solve and prove formulae.

The formula system is the most popular today, but when we asked survey participants to indicate which new system they would select, 36 percent (140 of the 387 respondents) did not select the formula method. Rather, they prefer the pay for performance method by a margin of 2 to 1. The formula method was the second highest preferred response with 18 percent (71 respondents). While the formula method has been the method of choice in the past, there is a definite trend toward the pay for performance method.

Those who favor a formula system generally argue it is relatively simple to implement and saves management time when it comes to making compensation decisions. Gather the information (for example, billable hours, new business generation, collections, and book of business), enter it into the formula, and then, *voilá*, the compensation distribution issue is over. Or is it? These are definitely pluses.

Although the formula system can be easy to apply and may decrease compensation-related discussions, there are, however, inherent problems in this system. First, we have seen many formulas that do not recognize or reward all the criteria necessary for the firm's long-term success and growth. Many simple formula plans tend to ignore intangible criteria (for example, training, mentoring, and developing new service areas) and merely focus on the tangible criteria (for example, collections, billable hours, and new business).

A good formula system should recognize tangible and intangible (long-term, capacity-building) factors in a balanced fashion.

Second, while formulas are easy to administer, they are also easy to manipulate. Formulas that reward charge time (not billable time) are perhaps the easiest to manipulate. Look at a common flaw based on the experiences of one firm.

ABC firm was using a formula that rewards chargeable hours. One of the owners, who worked the system, annually charged 1,800 hours but billed only half of them. Another owner in the firm charged 1,400 hours and billed 95 percent of them. The second owner contributed more to the bottom line of the firm than the first, but, per the formula, the first was paid more based on the chargeable hour factor.

Another owner in the same firm, the so-called rainmaking owner, also realized he could manipulate another of the factors. Because the formula was heavily weighted toward new business brought into the firm, this owner developed significant new business, but it was not profitable business. Because client profitability was not a key measure, this owner, like the one above, was arguably overpaid.

There is one thing you can be sure about: owners are smart, and if there is a way to work the system, some will be tempted to do so. That is why, no matter what compensation system you ultimately use, it should measure and reward the right activities for your firm.

Third, while firms like formulas for their simplicity, a good formula system needs to have some flexibility. It cannot be as simple as 1 + 2 = 3. What does the firm do when there are special circumstances, such as a short-term illness or a personal issue? And how does the firm treat an owner who turns a money-losing niche into a success when it is not part of the formula?

Fourth, if you use a strict formula in determining owner compensation, you may limit management's ability to manage the firm, that is, to reward or to discipline. A good formula system should be a *guide* to setting compensation, not a policy. It needs subjective elements so management can reward exceptional behavior or send a message for substandard behavior. Many of the formula systems we have seen contain subjective elements that can make up as much as 50 percent of the total compensation package or bonus element.

According to L. Gary Boomer, a well-known consultant to the accounting profession, a formula approach tends to work best in firms with 10 owners or fewer. This concept is outlined in Exhibit 7–2, "Compensation Systems by Firm Size—Boomer." This does not mean larger firms do not, or cannot successfully use this method. It is not necessarily the size of the firm that determines whether this method is used; it is the culture. Firms that previously operated as silos will often use a formula system. They have generally sustained independent practices with little desire to bring other owners' talents to individual client bases. We will discuss this further when we look at the *eat what you kill* method.

We also often see a formula approach in firms that are moving from an equal pay system or are transitioning from the first generation of owners to the second, and especially when the firm's first managing owner behaved somewhat dictatorially and made most compensation decisions. In many cases, this is a logical next step in the firm's compensation evolution. These firms usually set up a formula that rewards finders (those who bring in business), minders (those who supervise accounts and grow them), and grinders (those who sit behind their desks and produce). Profits are allocated to these three types of contributors, and the firm needs to weight the value of each group's contributions.

While firms will generally weight each group's contributions differently, it is often best to simply allocate 33.3 percent to each group. The example in Exhibit 7–3, "Sample Finders, Minders, and Grinders Allocation," shows how this would work in a firm. In the example, Owner A received 38 percent of the profits, Owner B received 22 percent, Owner C received 24 percent, and Owner D received 16 percent. If any one owner wants to increase his or her share of the profits in the coming year, he or she knows what to do. This type of compensation system can have complete transparency.

Whatever you decide, it is important to clearly define the allocation method and establish a formula that is fair and acceptable to the owners. This will go a long way toward avoiding annual disputes. Firms that use a formula method generally do not change the weighting often. Our experience suggests that changing a compensation system too often can lead to the dissolution of the firm. Two examples of effective use of the formula method are included in Exhibit 7–4, "Simple Unit Formula," and Exhibit 7–5, "Law Firm Formula."

EQUAL PAY METHOD

Thomas Jefferson may have captured it best when he said, "There is nothing more unequal than the equal treatment of unequal people." And that's the problem with an equal pay system.

This system generally works best when firms are just starting out and there are two to four (that is, a small number of) owners. (See Exhibits 7–1, 7–2, and 7–3 at end of this chapter). Equal pay is an easy way for owners to dodge the compensation bullet, and it usually implies that owners are afraid or do not want to have open and honest discussions about sensitive issues, deal with performance issues, or determine the relative value each owner brings to the firm. Although not always the case, these firms often lack a strong-willed or driving managing owner.

Firms that accept this approach usually have a cohesive group of owners with similar work ethics and client service philosophies, or they haven't taken adequate time to identify what is important as a firm and what they want to reward. This system assumes everyone's contribution is equal and works as long as all owners put forth equal effort and relatively equal results. However, when reality sets in, owners often realize they bring different skills, talents, commitment, and results to the practice.

As soon as one or more owners believe they contribute more than others, compensation problems start to arise. If we were going to create a continuum of compensation systems based on number of criteria and appropriateness of the criteria, the equal pay would be at the far left because there is no performance criteria used to determine compensation.

This system can be detrimental to a firm's long-term health for the following reasons:

- It creates a culture of mediocrity.
- There is generally no incentive for any one owner to perform at a higher level than others.
- There may be no individual recognition for a job well done.
- It often hinders the firm's growth.
- It limits the firm's ability to be profitable.
- It often drives out high performers.

If we begin to get the picture that this system is so bad, why did it rank as the second most popular in our survey? There are likely several reasons:

- Of the 67 firms that have an equal pay system, 49 of them have four owners or fewer.
- This system creates a collegial culture, especially in smaller firms.
- Equal pay plans are easy to implement.
- Owners with similar work ethics—whatever they might be—often embrace this type of plan.

While equal pay is not the plan of choice for larger firms, many smaller firms find that it works just right for them.

LOCKSTEP METHOD

While we did not include a variation of equal pay method as a choice in our survey, it is often seen in law firms and is generally called the lockstep method. The lockstep income distribution system embodies a philosophy of equal sharing of income among those owners who are at the same level of tenure with the firm, without being overly concerned about their exact contributions. It rewards individual owners based on longevity. It is a variation of the equal pay method in that employees who become owners at the same time keep their income distribution in lock step.

It is based on the assumption (perhaps a false one) that the longer an individual is an owner, the more valuable he or she becomes to the firm. This system has worked well for many law firms and some accounting firms. With the trend toward the pay for performance method, however, the lock step method is becoming scarcer, even in law firms. We believe the reason is simple. Owners who embrace this method are usually not entrepreneurial or aggressive. Younger owners are willing to wait their turn to grab the golden ring.

At one extreme, this income distribution system can be detrimental to a firm's long-term health. Assume for a moment it does not reward for current production or for building future capacity. Owners merely show up to receive a paycheck. In this scenario, you find owners who have retired but have failed to tell anyone. As the saying goes, nice work if you can get it.

In reality, the lockstep method does require that certain performance levels must be achieved for the owner to participate fully in the income opportunities, and there is an overriding philosophy that the individual owner contributions need to be reasonably equal.

This type of system usually works best in small firms with owners who are similar in age. There may have been three or four owners that started the firm under an equal pay plan, and as the next group of owners entered the practice, the second group maintains its own equal pay plan.

A positive aspect of this plan is that it forms a cohesive group out of the various owner tiers (as long as they have similar values and work production). As with any of the plans we discuss, this one works especially well when the firm is very profitable. With enough dollars to pass around, it is easier for owners to overlook another's mediocre or poor performance.

HYBRID APPROACH METHOD

Fifty-five firms responded to our first question ("What type of owner compensation system does the firm currently use?") by checking the "other" category rather than any of the other 10 categories. Our belief is *other* means these firms are using hybrid compensation methods. In other words, they use elements from one or more of the other methods. Because the responses varied across the board, we share them here so you see how firms take elements from various methods to create an approach that works for them.

For example, several respondents in this category use the equal pay method, except that the managing owner receives an additional stipend for managing the firm. Another firm uses the equal pay formula but deducts $50 per hour for excessive time off. This firm also rewards owners for working excessive hours. One firm that uses an equal pay method also uses an ownership allocation. One provides equal pay plus a bonus (equal to one-fourth of his or her production) to the partner with the highest billings. Another has equal base pay of $72,000, and profits over that amount are allocated by a formula that measures *contact* and *managed* volume.

Many firms use an algebraic formula that includes elements of pay for performance, ownership percentage, and managing owner prerogative. One firm used a 75 percent formula approach and 25 percent for performance. Still another respondent indicated his or her firm uses a combination of formula, guaranteed payment, and subjective allocation by the compensation committee. One respondent wrote, "We use a combination of formula, ownership, and achievement of firm goals. Fifty percent is firm goal achievement, 25 percent profitability (formula), and 25 percent ownership. Last year's goal was growth of practice."

Some firms used a combination of compensation committee and ownership percentage. The compensation committee sets the annual salary or draw, and owners receive a monthly interest payment on accrual-based capital. At the end of the year, owners are eligible for a subjective bonus. After all payments are made, remaining dollars go toward profit sharing based on ownership.

One firm provided the following, "Our base pay is determined by past history and present responsibilities. It is different for each partner. Firm profits are then split as follows: first 25 percent (but not less than $50,000) stays in the company, second 25 percent is by ownership, and third 25 percent discretionary by compensation committee (with each partner giving input for extraordinary matters done during the year be it monetary or nonmonetary). The final 25 percent is split equally amongst all owners."

MANAGING OWNER DECIDES METHOD

Because the formula method can produce the wrong results and misguided incentives, many firms add subjective elements to the formula or move to a completely subjective approach wherein the managing owner makes all the compensation decisions, perhaps with some input.

When the managing owner makes all compensation decisions, the system is simple and is generally based on the following principle that the benevolent dictator espouses: "Trust me . . . I certainly know what everyone is worth."

A system in which one person makes all compensation decisions tends to work best in smaller firms where the managing owner is the founder and also the major shareholder. In this scenario, most of the other owners are playing the roles of highly paid managers and have resigned themselves to the reality that authority remains with the managing owner.

In our survey, 33 firms indicated they use this method. Of the 33 firms, 26 have four owners or fewer, and six firms have from five to nine owners. Only one firm had 10 or more owners.

Leaving such an important decision to one person can create a host of problems for the firm and its owners. Consider the following situations:

- Owners may have abdicated their rights to discuss compensation issues.
- Because owners are often not allowed to discuss compensation, this may breed a low degree of trust among them.
- Firms that let a single individual determine everyone's compensation usually have a larger gap between the highest and lowest paid owner.

Our survey shows the following:

- Owners under this scenario usually do not work as a team because one of the basic principles for developing a strong team is open and emotional discussion that leads to good conclusions.
- The managing owner may justify his or her worth and compensate himself or herself the most, or he or she may overcompensate specific owners to avoid conflicts or minimize the disappointment of these owners.
- The benevolent managing owner may have his or her favorites and compensate them accordingly.

ALL OWNERS DECIDE METHOD

We have heard some people say the "last man standing" method (all owners meet as a group and decide) is more than a compensation system, it is often a "free-for-all" or "blood bath." When owners get together to determine each other's compensation, there is generally one of two outcomes. Owners have an open and robust discussion about each other's contributions and shortcomings and leave the meeting feeling good about individual and firm outcomes. Or, they have a shouting match, and the owner who screams the loudest and longest often wins.

If facilitated in the right spirit, the all owners decide method is an excellent way for owners to help each other see areas of needed improvement. If not, it can be very emotional and destructive to the firm.

Many times this system does not include preestablished goals for owners. Hence everyone scrambles at the end of the year to record their lists of accomplishments. It often becomes evident that individual accomplishments are not guided by common vision and strategic goals. For this system to work, it is critical for each owner to have a list of goals and objectives that are determined at the beginning of the year.

Our survey suggests this system generally works well for smaller firms, that is, those with 10 or fewer owners.

OWNERSHIP PERCENTAGE METHOD

We have observed more and more firms bifurcating compensation from ownership. In other words, relative compensation levels no longer track with ownership levels. Firms that tie ownership directly to compensation are usually making a mistake. While equity is important when it comes to selling a practice, apportioning the capital needs of the firm, and establishing voting rights in the management of the firm, equity should not be a primary factor in determining compensation. Marc Rosenberg commented in "Not All Owners Are Created Equal":

> Compensation for ownership and compensation for performance should be dealt with separately. Many firms provide for payments to retired owners. These payments typically are not guaranteed, and they remunerate owners for a number of things, chief among them being ownership in the firm and the value and size of the client base they originated. The mistake many firms make is mixing together ownership and performance in determining annual income allocations.[1]

Therefore, we would disagree with the following statement: "If I own 50 percent of the firm, I deserve 50 percent of the profits." Determining compensation based on ownership is an entitlement program, similar to seniority. Most firms that use this method are small, with one or two owners who hold most of the equity.

In these firms, owners may take small amounts of compensation during the year, and then distribute profits based on ownership. Obviously, minority owners are not incentivized to bring in new business because they receive only a small percentage (equal to ownership) of the new business net revenue.

This system has problems similar to any entitlement system:

- It does not encourage owners to develop new services or talents.
- It does not encourage younger owners to work hard or build the practice.
- It encourages mediocrity.
- It can hinder the growth of the firm.
- It does not maximize profitability.
- It does not reward individuals for performance.

We asked a few well-known consultants about ownership percentage affecting owner compensation. Marc Rosenberg said, "It doesn't. That's it. Everything relating to annual compensation should be performance based." Don Scholl told us, "A return on capital is not the same thing as compensation and should be handled as an expense of the business.

---

[1]Marc L. Rosenberg, "Not All Partners Are Created Equal: Essential Elements of an Effective Partner Compensation System," *Insight* (May 1977): 9.

Owner compensation should primarily be related to that individual's total contribution to the firm's current success."

Chris Frederiksen agreed with Marc and Don. "I see many firms where the lion's share of the pie is divided based on ownership with little regard being given to individual performance. What this does is disenfranchise the younger owners who can only realistically improve their income through superior performance. Also, sooner or later, it causes grief in the firm; the high performing owner will feel under-compensated and the under-performing owner has no way to gracefully take less money." To read more of these interviews, see Exhibit 7–6, "Interview With High Profile Consultants About Owner Compensation," at the end of this chapter.

PAY FOR PERFORMANCE METHOD

A real pay for performance program aligns owner and employee compensation to the firm's strategic initiatives. The fact that many accounting firms today do not have clearly defined strategic objectives can explain in part why only 5.4 percent of the respondents to our 2006 Compensation Survey listed a pay for performance method. However, if you want to drive superior results (performance) in your firm, align owner and employee compensation to the firm's strategic initiatives. We discuss this method thoroughly throughout the book.

EAT WHAT YOU KILL METHOD

If this sounds like a barbaric system, it is! An *eat what you kill* system rewards the hunter's individual efforts, and everyone is essentially on their own. This is a simplified type of formula approach in that bringing in business and doing the work are the primary activities; nothing else matters in this compensation system. In this system, earnings are directly proportional to the business an owner brings in and executes. In a group practice, there is no cash reserve to provide a draw or salary when an owner and his team are not billable. And to keep one's production up, there is major emphasis on bringing in new business and hoarding the business you already have. When individuals keep the spoils of their hunt, teamwork is thwarted.

As with each system we discuss in this book, of course, there may be variations in the *eat what you kill* approach to compensation. Each owner often pays a share of overhead and is charged for all or some of the salaries of employees who work for him or her. Because owners are directly responsible for the costs of employees who work for them, they are likely to hire hard working team members. This is one of the good points of this system.

Another strong point of the system is that owners know exactly what they must do to achieve their desired incomes. This is similar to the formula system we discussed above. To survive under this system, therefore, owners need to bring in business. If an owner does not get paid what he or she wants, he or she has no one to blame but himself or herself. Owners under this system are also very conscientious about receivables. Unless they collect *on* them, they are not compensated *for* them.

A final positive about this system is the need for almost no management time to determine compensation because each owner essentially determines his or her own compensation.

While there are a number of positive points, this system is not without problems. Many times it is difficult to get owners to spend time managing the firm, especially if there is no recognition for nonbillable time. Individual owners may train individuals who work under them, but there is generally no firm-wide consistency in training and development. In an *eat what you kill* environment, staff members often need to be self-starters because there is either inconsistent or little training support.

There are also problems with sharing staff members in an *eat what you kill* environment. Employees are often required to learn new processes and procedures because owners often set up their files differently and approach engagements in their own unique fashion. Cross-servicing does not usually happen because owners are more interested in feeding themselves than others.

Firms that follow an *eat what you kill* compensation system have owners who operate independently yet under the same roof. This is often called *operating in silos*. Owners in these firms do not need to have relationships with each other because they depend on themselves for success. This, in turn, often hinders the firm in maximizing profitability. The *eat what you kill* method does not contribute to building a firm of the future because total emphasis is on the here and now. A Generation X employee may tolerate this environment, but Generation Y employees may rebel because they are generally more team oriented.

COMPENSATION COMMITTEE METHOD

Our study suggests that a compensation system in which a compensation committee determines base pay and bonus is generally employed only when the firm has seven or more owners. If there are fewer than seven owners, it probably does not make as much sense to consider this method. While smaller firms sometimes use compensation committees, they generally move to *consensus* because they probably want to have at least 3 owners on the committee. As the number of owners grows to 10 or more, so grows the use of compensation committees.

Having a compensation committee make decisions may be preferable to having only the managing owner make decisions, provided all members of the committee are not founding owners. Also, when there is more than one person involved in determining profit allocation and even base salary, the allocation tends to be fairer. Compensation committees can often be fairer than executive committees because different members of the firm can be elected to the committee each year, whereas executive committees tend to be more stable in their membership.

Seldom does a compensation committee base its decisions purely on subjective factors. Most firms gather detailed statistics on each owner, and members of the compensation committee review the statistics prior to making decisions. The compensation committee usually interviews each owner, considers objective management reports or self evaluation reports, and makes a recommendation to the executive committee or ownership group as a whole. Depending on firm size, firm type, and the make-up of the owners, the compensation committee approach can work well.

Compensation committee membership can take on many forms, and we recommend that its membership mirror the diversity of the owner group. Larger single-office firms will also have representation from different departments within the firm (for example, tax, audit, and consulting), and multioffice firms will have representation from different regions. It is important that the committee make-up be composed of management plus one or two other owners who are elected by the remaining owners. An ideal committee make-up may consist of an owner who represents each generation of owners, plus the managing owner. Having the proper mixture of owners provides greater credibility to the committee and usually results in allocations that are fair.

Karen MacKay, a consultant with Edge International, one of the premier consulting firms to the legal profession, believes a good compensation committee should also be made up of different personality types. In her article, "Selecting the Compensation Committee: The Power of Balancing Personalities," MacKay suggests that selection of committee members take into consideration the Myers Briggs Type Indicator (MBTI)®.[2]

"MBTI measures our orientation of energy—where we get our energy. This is known as the E-I Dichotomy. If you prefer introversion, you draw energy from the inside. You prefer to communicate in writing. You prefer to take the time to reflect on the issues and work out your ideas in your head. You think through the issues. If you prefer extroversion you draw energy from the external environment. You prefer to communicate by talking. You work best by doing and discussing, in short you talk through the issues."

A balance of introverts and extroverts will enable the committee to both think through and talk through the critical issues. The introverts will give careful, thoughtful, reflective consideration while the extroverts will be sure the group has put the issues on the table—they will pull the thoughts out of the others on the committee until they are satisfied. Designing the format for the compensation committee's deliberations requires sensitivity to the energy needs of the participants. Four days of straight meetings is tiring for anyone, but it will literally "suck the life out of the introverts. They need breathing space. They need reflective, alone time to be effective."[3]

Now, think about your compensation committee.

---

[2] *Edge International Review*, Winter 2005.
[3] Karen MacKay, "Selecting the Compensation Committee: The Power of Balancing Personalities," *Edge International Review*, Winter 2005.

EXECUTIVE COMMITTEE METHOD

The executive committee approach is similar to the compensation committee approach. The primary difference is that members of the executive committee are often more senior members of the firm or the largest rainmakers.

A major drawback of this method, similar to a compensation committee, is that the executive committee also determines its own members' compensation. We have found it is not unusual for the executive committee to recommend compensation for the managing owner, but determining its own compensation can be problematic. Perhaps you could form a compensation committee to determine compensation for executive committee members!

PEN AND PAPER METHOD

The pen and paper method of determining compensation and bonuses is fairly simple and often used by smaller firms. There are several variations to this method, but the method generally works like this. Each owner is given a sheet of paper that lists all of the owners' names as well as the total dollar amount that will be allocated for bases and bonuses. The owners then allocate the dollars among all owners, including themselves. The managing owner or firm administrator tabulates the results to obtain an average for each owner.

The individual recommendations can certainly remain a secret. In other words, owners may see what other owners have recommended, but they do not know who made which recommendation. We call this the *chicken method*. A variation of the chicken method is the *open method*, in which owners know who recommended what. The benefit of this open method is that it allows for robust dialogue among owners about why they made specific recommendations.

Exhibit 7–7, "Sample Owner Compensation and Bonus Allocation Input Form," shows what a sample individual input sheet would look like. In this case, there are four owners in the firm, and they have $1,000,000 to allocate ($800,000 in base pay and $200,000 in bonuses).

Depending on the number of owners in the firm, the highest and lowest recommended allocation could be discarded when determining the average. This type of method can also be used to gain input for an executive or compensation committee and for the managing owner decides method.

To help owners determine their recommended allocations, many firms distribute to each owner key measures and other statistics. These usually come from an owner self-evaluation form.

FINAL THOUGHTS

There are 40 firms, and each has a different compensation method or system, and each compensation method has a profound influence on the firm's success or failure. So, what do you do now? Simply changing from one compensation method to another is certainly not the answer.

Designing a compensation system that is right for your firm requires a detailed assessment and design (or redesign) of your mission, vision, values, and strategy to make sure the system is exactly right for your firm.

Each firm needs to determine what it values most and why this makes your firm unique. The basic question to ask and answer is, "What do owners want to accomplish, and what compensation system will help us do this?"

EXHIBIT 7–1

Compensation Systems by Firm Size—Rosenberg

	2 Owners	3–4 Owners	5–7 Owners	8–11 Owners	12+ Owners
Compensation committee	0	5%	18%	24%	50%
Formula	23%	56%	42%	48%	36%
Paper and pencil	0	2%	6%	10%	5%
Ownership percentage	16%	9%	4%	0	9%
MP decides	13%	11%	14%	7%	0
Equal pay	35%	4%	8%	7%	0
All owners decide	13%	13%	8%	4%	0

Source: The Rosenberg Survey, 2005, p 17

EXHIBIT 7–2   **Compensation Systems by Firm Size—Boomer**

System	2–3 Owners	4–7 Owners	8–10 Owners	>10 owners
Equal	Common	Rare	Never	Never
Formula	Common	Very common	Less common	Seldom
Spreadsheet	Rare	Effective at upper end	Can work	Too difficult
MP decision	Rare	Can work well	Becomes difficult	More difficult
Compensation committee	No	No	Becomes viable	Common
Points/units	No	No	No	Still in use
Balanced scorecard	Will work in any size firm with proper leadership, governance and a Strategic plan			

Gary Boomer, *Owner Compensation*, published by Boomer Consulting

EXHIBIT 7–3   **Sample Finders, Minders, and Grinders Allocation**

Owner Statistics

Type of contributor	Weighting	Owner A	Owner B	Owner C	Owner D
Finder origination	33.3	$200,000	$ 40,000	$100,000	$ 25,000
Minder book	33.3	$ 1.2m	$460,000	$600,000	$260,000
Grinder billable $	33.3	$ 40,000	$315,000	$200,000	$325,000

Owner Profit Sharing

Type of Contributor	Weighting	Owner A	Owner B	Owner C	Owner D	Total	% of Total
Finder origination	33.3	$ 66,600	$ 13,320	$ 33,300	$ 8,325	$ 121,545	10%
Minder book	33.3	$399,600	$153,180	$199,800	$ 85,580	$ 838,160	67%
Grinder billable $	33.3	$ 13,320	$104,895	$ 66,600	$108,225	$ 293,040	23%
Totals	100%	$479,520	$271,395	$299,700	$202,130	$1,252,745	100%
% of Total		38%	22%	24%	16%	100%	

EXHIBIT 7–4   **Simple Unit Formula**

In "Partner Compensation Systems in Professional Services Firms Part II," Michael Andersen shares, "The simple unit formula is designed to reward seniority, production, client generation and non-billable activities, using a relatively straightforward and totally objective calculation. A typical formula might be that each owner receives:

- One unit/point for each year with the firm
- One unit/point for $x of production (fees billed or fees received)
- One unit/point for x of client generation.

The non-billable units/points are awarded on the basis that the total available number of units/points is three times the number of owners. Then, those available units/points are allocated on a pro rata basis for non-billable time recorded. Needless to say, when all of the units/points have been allocated, they are converted to percentages and then applied to the net firm profit for the fiscal year to create each owner's individual income.

This system is not unlike the modified Hale and Dorr system in that it mainly rewards production in an objective manner. The biggest differences are that the simple unit formula also rewards longevity with the firm as well as some non-billable efforts."

Source: Michael J. Andersen, "Partner Compensation Systems in Professional Services Firms Part II," http://www.edge.ai/Edge-International-1057907.html; 2007, Edge International, accessed on January 25, 2007.

EXHIBIT 7–5 **Law Firm Formula**

The law firm of Flaster Greenberg is one of New Jersey's largest law firms, with 60 attorneys and 7 offices in New Jersey, Pennsylvania, and Delaware. The firm posts the following on its Web site (www.flastergreenberg.com).

"Unlike most law firms, shareholder compensation is not determined by a subset of shareholders; but rather, by an objective formula equally applied to all shareholders. The mechanics of the formula are discussed below. The effect on the Firm of having this form of compensation system is dramatic. The typical politics present at many firms is absent. New shareholders need not worry about alliances, voting blocks or existing loyalties among more senior attorneys. Management and the shareholders are not preoccupied with compensation issues and instead focus on strategic decisions. Shareholders are content because they feel like owners and are confident every shareholder is treated equally.

As discussed above, shareholder compensation is determined by an objective formula. Our compensation formula tracks each shareholder's *production* (cash collected on a shareholder's time), client responsibility or *minding* (cash collected on files that the shareholder manages) and *originations* (cash collected on files originated by the shareholder).

Each year, the shareholders determine the total amount available for distribution. Twenty five percent (25%) of this amount is then allocated proportionately to the shareholders based on origination, nineteen percent (19%) is allocated proportionately to the shareholders based on client responsibility and fifty six percent (56%) is allocated to the shareholders proportionately based on production.

Each shareholder is provided reports showing these figures for all attorneys. All financial information at the Firm is shared with every shareholder. The administration of the compensation formula involves quite an extensive spreadsheet and the firm has modified the formula to address contingent fees, associate profit and certain firm service by shareholders; however, the formula is applied equally to each shareholder. The primary benefits of the compensation formula are:

- Shareholders receive the same production credit regardless of whether they work on a client file they originated or another attorney's file.
- The typical credit for origination is divided into two categories origination and client responsibility to allow for sharing between attorneys. Accordingly, an attorney is rewarded for bringing in a client to the firm and where another shareholder manages the file; the minding attorney(s) is rewarded for servicing and growing the client.
- All politics associated with compensation are removed from the Firm.
- The delicate balance between rewarding originators and rewarding the working attorneys is maintained as evidenced by the fact that both the Firm's high originators and high billers have remained at the Firm.
- Our compensation formula recognizes the varying contributions of all shareholders and the Firm does not need to differentiate shareholders by de-equitizing all but the highest originators."

Source: "The Flaster/Greenberg Difference," http://www.flastergreenberg.com/careers/flaster difference.cfm; 2006, Flaster/Greenberg, accessed on January 25, 2007.

EXHIBIT 7–6   **Interview With High-Profile Consultants About Owner Compensation[4]**

Partner Advantage Advisory (PAA): All firms at one time or another ponder the following questions, and there must be as many different ways to respond as there are firms. But, just because a firm has a way of doing something, does not make it right or the best way. So when we think about the following questions, there are two ways that each one of you can respond:

- What are firms doing?
- What *should* firms be doing?

Here are the questions that firms should be asking:

1. How much accrual basis capital should a firm maintain?
2. Why is equity so important?
3. When admitting a new owner, how does the firm decide how much ownership (equity percentage) to assign to that person? If a person becomes a 5 percent owner, this is 5 percent of what?
4. What is the purpose of requiring new owners to buy in?
5. To where does the new owner buy-in amount get paid?
6. Should owners receive some return on their capital investment?
7. How should ownership percentage affect owner compensation?
8. How should ownership percentage affect owner retirement?
9. How should owners vote? One man-one vote or by ownership percentage?
10. Should quality review findings and/or regulatory agency disciplinary actions effect owner compensation?

How much accrual basis capital should a firm maintain? Owners are making greater investments in technology, real estate, and marketing than ever before. It seems that new owners and even existing owners only want to take money out of the firm. They often find it hard to think of a practice like a real business where you buy assets, pay people, and make investments for the future. What are you seeing the market today? How are firms determining capital accounts? What's the rationale behind their methods and how are owners coping with keeping more money in their firms?

Bob Martin: Before the question is answered, it's important to understand that for most firms, accrual basis capital is mostly WIP and A/R.

Don Scholl: No matter if the firm is a sole practitioner or multioffice, multiowner entity, each firm should require some capital to fund its working capital needs and any capital requirements for equipment and property. I have always felt that, at a minimum, capital accounts should be 20 percent of a firm's budgeted collections. This minimum anticipates that the firm will be using its line of credit for some part of the year.

Further, there is a positive element about having a low capital requirement. It can force the owners to become aggressive in collecting accounts receivable.

Marc Rosenberg: Sophisticated firms will set a target for capital. The most common target is a percentage of net fees, usually 20 percent to 30 percent. But the vast majority of firms are not this formal and do not set any target for capital. Capital is as it is. The key, from a cash flow or capital-planning standpoint, is to avoid paying compensation to owners before WIP and A/R is collected.

---

[4]"The Role of Ownership: A Roundtable Discussion" Reprinted with permission from *Partner Advantage Advisory* 2, no. 5 (May 2004): 2 and 4.

August Aquila: I've noticed that the aggressive and growth oriented firms require owners to contribute 30 percent or more of collected fees. This provides the firm with the needed capital to make investments in new services or ventures.

Chris Frederiksen: I've seen a few firms go as high as 50 percent of fees. But that is surely not the norm. In any case, the capital should at least equal the net income of the firm before any owner compensation. With regards to Don Scholl's comment, I would recommend to a million dollar firm with net income of $350,000 to have at least that $350,000 in capital.

Bob Martin: I would add to Chris's net income principle above, that total amount should be allocated among owners according to their compensation, set at 1.0 or more times individual compensation.

PAA: Why is equity so important?

Marc Rosenberg: Equity is important especially when a firm is sold, when an owner retires and in some cases, in voting. Voting will be addressed later. When a firm is sold or an owner retires, there are usually two payments made—capital and goodwill. When either of these two events occurs, the owner receives their share of the equity as well as the return of their capital as outlined in the owner's agreement.

Steve Erickson: Problems arise at firms when equity is used too heavily for owner compensation or owner retirement purposes. Benefits should be awarded based upon what each owner contributed to the creation of the earnings, in the case of compensation, and to the creation of goodwill, in the case of retirement.

PAA: When admitting a new owner, how does the firm decide how much ownership (equity percentage) to assign to that person? If a person becomes a 5 percent owner, this is 5 percent of what?

August Aquila: That's an interesting question. Assume that the existing owner agrees that the new owner should have 10 percent equity interest in the firm. First, I think you have to determine if that means 10 percent of the earnings, then you need to decide if it is on the cash or accrual basis. Then there is the issue of goodwill. To get a true picture of the value of a firm, real businesses use accrual basis financial statements.

Marc Rosenberg: This is one of the most comical and haphazard areas of CPA firm practice management. Most firms, if they were honest, would admit that there has been no coherent or consistent system used to determine ownership percentage. This is a big mistake because if ownership is used in important ways, like allocating income or determining retirement benefits, it will make the owners very unhappy when the inevitable arises: an owner with a high ownership percentage is awarded compensation or retirement benefits that are far in excess of what he deserves.

Bob Martin: We should remember that ownership percentage has an impact on owners in five possible ways:

1. Voting
2. Compensation
3. Retirement benefits
4. Determining buy-in amount
5. Allocating assets and liabilities from the sale or liquidation of the firm

But, the impact and influence of ownership percentage can be eliminated in all but number five above.

Steve Erickson: The larger the role that ownership plays on the above, the more problems and complications you will have. Conversely, if you minimize the role of ownership percentage, it makes it easier to bring in new owners and deal with each of the above areas separately.

Rita Keller: When it comes to compensation, it should be allocated primarily on the basis of performance, not ownership. However, there are still a lot of small firms paying senior owners on ownership.

Chris Frederiksen: I would add that retirement benefits should be determined based upon what each owner did to contribute to the creation of the firm's value. Bringing in clients is just one way to contribute to the value; other ways such as firm management, staff development, technical expertise, and so on, should also play important roles.

Don Scholl: Buy-in should be determined not by ownership percentage, but by what the current owners feel is a meaningful number that they want each new owner to contribute. For example, take the case of a four owner, $3 million firm with capital of $1 million. If you admit a fifth owner and want that person to be a 5 percent owner, that would result in a buy-in amount of $200,000, which today, is considered by most firms to be higher than what young people are willing to pay. The firm is better off deciding on a meaningful amount, say $50,000, and working backward to decide on the ownership percentage. In this case, the new owner would own 1.2 percent of the firm (50,000 divided by 4,050,000).

PAA: What is the purpose of requiring new owners to buy in?

Marc Rosenberg: The theory is that all owners should feel that they have a meaningful amount of money invested in the firm that is at risk. The firm is a valuable asset that is relatively liquid. Why would any owner of a valuable, liquid asset, "give away" its ownership?

Steve Erickson: Owners have to show their willingness to put their money at risk. It's one of the major tenets of ownership. Even if they don't fund their capital accounts at once, they should be fully funded by the end of five years.

Bob Martin: I can tell you one thing, when someone goes to the bank and takes a loan to make his or her capital contribution, there is more of a commitment to the firm. The title of owner now means a lot more.

August Aquila: Years ago when I was an owner in a CPA firm, not only did I feel committed, I always felt that the firm had some leverage over me and other owners if we decided to leave the firm and set up shop across the street. Having a significant capital account at risk surely makes owners think twice before leaving a firm.

Don Scholl: Where else would the firm find funding for its operations? I guess it could go to the bank. But I'm not sure why a bank would provide funds to a small under capitalized firm that had no capital in it.

Chris Frederiksen: Having money at stake is only equitable if you are going to share in the rewards of ownership. Normally the amount of money invested has a relationship to the amount of money you earn. Many firms adjust your investment based on your relative share of the firm's net income.

PAA: To where does the new owner buy-in amount get paid?

Rita Keller: Buy-in amounts should be paid to the firm. Most firms find that new owner buy-ins are a simple way of financing the growth of the firm and to finance the capital payments to retired owners that are replaced by the new owners.

Marc Rosenberg: This is an aspect of this whole topic that is mishandled by many firms. Many firms have the buy-ins of new owners paid to the existing owners. This isn't fair to the new owner for the following reasons:

1. He has nothing to show for it on the firm's balance sheet. Someone cannot look at the firm's balance sheet and determine who paid in capital to the firm.
2. If there is a return on capital segment of the compensation system, as there should be, he won't get any of this.

Payment of a buy-in amount to existing owners really is an advance payment of that owner's retirement benefits. Yet, the way many firms work it, the new owner gets no credit for these payments in determining *their* retirement benefits.

PAA: Should owners receive some return on their capital investment?

Marc Rosenberg: There is no doubt that a CPA firm is a valuable earning asset whose value is relatively liquid. Investors in any investment should be entitled to a reasonable return on their investment.

Chris Frederiksen: Buy-in amounts should definitely be paid to the firm and *not* to the retiring individual. There are already enough opportunities for conflict in these situations without creating new ones.

PAA: How should ownership percentage affect owner retirement?

Marc Rosenberg: Not at all. Retirement benefits should be determined based upon what each owner has contributed to the value of the firm.

Chris Frederiksen: Retirement benefits should be based on what the retiring owner has contributed to the firm over his or her career. There are two common ways of measuring this: (A) By the book of business an owner has amassed and leaves with the firm. For example, a firm might pay out 80 percent of the owner's retained business over a 10-year period (that is, 8 percent of collections each year for 10 years) and (B) by the owner's compensation level. For example, a firm might calculate the average of an owner's highest 3 years of compensation occurring within the last 10 years. The firm might then pay out 25 percent of this amount each year for 10 years. Some firms pay the *higher* of (A) or (B) and some firms pay the *lower* of the two. Which one you pick will depend on your circumstances and what you are trying to accomplish.

PAA: How should owners vote? One man gets one vote, or by ownership percentage?

August Aquila: This is another complicated area. For the most part, problems are avoided if you vote on a one-man-one-vote basis. When votes are taken on an ownership percentage basis, it disenfranchises the lower owners, makes them feel like they are not an owner. They almost literally have no vote.

Marc Rosenberg: The biggest argument for voting on an ownership basis is one in which control is an issue. Take the situation where there are one or two founding/long-time owners. Now they admit a few new owners who clearly don't have the wherewithal of the established owners. Obviously, the older owners don't want to expose themselves to being kicked out of their own firm by a one-man-one-vote system.

Chris Frederiksen: There are two ways to deal with this:

1. All votes are a one-man-one-vote basis, but any owner reserves the right to vote by percentage if he so chooses (that is, doesn't like the way the first vote came out).
2. Stay with one-owner-one-vote, but establish a supermajority vote for key issues such as changing the owner agreement, mergers, firing an owner, etc.

EXHIBIT 7–7   **Sample Owner Compensation and Bonus Allocation Input Form**

Owner	Base Compensation Recommendation	Bonus Recommendation
A		
B		
C		
D		
TOTAL	$800,000	$200,000

Assume that Owner A completes the form and has allocated the dollars as follows:

Owner	Base Compensation Recommendation	Bonus Recommendation
A	$225,000	$ 75,000
B	$150,000	$ 20,000
C	$200,000	$ 50,000
D	$225,000	$ 55,000
TOTAL	$800,000	$200,000

Each of the other three owners completes the input sheet, and the final forms for compensation and bonus may look like the following:

Owner	Base Compensation Recommendation				Average
	A Recommendation	B Recommendation	C Recommendation	D Recommendation	
A	$225,000	$190,000	$205,000	$211,000	$207,750
B	$150,000	$158,000	$143,000	$152,000	$150,750
C	$200,000	$205,000	$196,000	$210,000	$202,750
D	$225,000	$247,000	$256,000	$227,000	$238,750
TOTAL	$800,000				$800,000

Owner	Bonus Compensation Recommendation				Average
	A Recommendation	B Recommendation	C Recommendation	D Recommendation	
A	$75,000	$56,000	$60,000	$66,000	$64,250
B	$20,000	$25,000	$22,000	$20,000	$21,750
C	$50,000	$50,000	$45,000	$55,000	$50,000
D	$55,000	$69,000	$73,000	$59,000	$64,000
TOTAL	$200,000				$200,000

CHAPTER 8

DESIGNING A NEW COMPENSATION SYSTEM: IT'S ABOUT PEOPLE

"Yes, compensation and incentives are important, but for very different reasons in good-to-great companies. The purpose of a compensation system should not be to get the right behaviors from the wrong people, but to get the right people on the bus in the first place, and to keep them there."

—Jim Collins

If you had the choice between the "right" compensation system and the "right" people, which would you choose? While we cannot answer for you, we can tell you we'd take the right people any day. In this chapter, we explain why a key to getting the right people is having a compensation system that attracts and retains them and to share ideas about how to get both. While the process we propose may not be perfect, it may increase your chances of making smart hiring decisions.

THE WAR FOR TALENT IS NOT OVER

Many would argue the war for talent is more intense than ever. Some would argue we are just now learning how to fight the war. According to the Bi-Annual PCPS MAP Top Five Issues Survey, finding and retaining top-quality staff is the most pressing obstacle for most firms. Ask any managing owner in any size CPA firm about his or her firm's greatest business challenge. He or she will likely tell you the number one issue facing the firm is a shortage of staff. And it's not just placing bodies at desks, but getting people who closely match the firm's culture (or desired culture) at those desks.

In 1998, readers were asked by The McKinsey Quarterly to answer the following two questions regarding their hiring and retention:

- Why would someone really want to join your organization?
- How will you keep them for more than a few years?

How would *you* answer these two questions? How would *your owners* answer them? Would their responses be consistent? How would *each employee* in your firm respond to the questions and how consistent would *their answers* be with one another's as well as your owners' answers?

When it comes to recruitment and retention, some firms focus effort on recruitment, while others focus effort on retention. Sadly, some focus on neither. But it's never really an either/or proposition. Firms, of course, need to focus on both! And individuals who are involved in recruitment and retention activities must be rewarded appropriately. In our consulting practices, we strive to help firms focus on retention by helping them develop programs in four areas:

- Creating a total compensation philosophy
- Becoming a great place to work
- Developing programs for growth opportunities
- Clarifying and working toward a compelling future

Creating a Total Compensation Philosophy

The key elements of a total compensation philosophy include the following issues:

- Fair pay
- Competitive benefits
- Incentives
- Rewards-for-results or pay-for-performance programs
- Recognition

Becoming a Great Place to Work

In many areas of the United States and Canada, public accounting firms are joining the lists of the "Best Places to Work." Those firms that make the list incorporate the following into their work environments:

- Increasing personal respect from and influence with others
- Creating an accepting, supportive, and teaming environment
- Creating a culture of empowering leaders
- Getting employees involved in decision-making
- Improving lines of communication
- Working on issues of work-life balance

Developing Programs for Growth Opportunities

It goes without saying that each firm needs to develop a program that satisfies the needs of its owners and staff. Investing in the development of hard and soft skills of its people is crucial for a firm's long-term success.

- Providing a learning environment (through workshops, coaching, or self-study, for example) at all levels of the firm that develops needed competencies
- Offering engaging and challenging work opportunities
- Providing a career progression path and career enhancement opportunities
- Establishing accountability mechanisms for both progress and results

Clarifying and Working Toward a Compelling Future

In the earlier chapters of this book we discussed mission, vision, and values. These are not just words written on a page. They are living elements that energize people in the firm and motivate them to do their best day-in and day-out:

- Instilling confidence in the firm's growth and success
- Taking pride in the firm's image and reputation
- Gaining confidence in the firm's products and services
- Sharing excitement about performing work that makes a difference
- Gaining a sense of accomplishment and contribution

Each of the above areas is key when it comes to recruitment and retention. Why? One of the reasons firms often do not retain people is they fail to deliver what was promised during the recruitment process. For example, recruits are often told during the recruitment process that employees are valued above clients—because, after all, without satisfied and loyal employees there would be no clients—only to find out the firm allows clients to mistreat its employees. Recruits are promised they will receive lots of client contact and challenging client assignments only to discover owners who hold client relationships and client work close to the vest.

To motivate firm members to engage in the proper behaviors, activities, and initiatives, firms must design their compensation systems accordingly. The owner who allows clients to mistreat the firm's employees and rarely provides employees the opportunity for client involvement should be given such feedback, and his or her compensation should be affected in light of other performance criteria. Likewise, the owner who involves team members regularly in client interaction and addresses inappropriate behavior on the part of a client toward employees should also be compensated accordingly.

One of the best tools to help you determine the ultimate systems and programs you should put into place is the book *First, Break all the Rules: What the World's Greatest Managers Do Differently*, by Marcus Buckingham and Curt Coffman.[1] In the book, the authors discuss the 12 things that matter to employees. The authors suggest the answer to the following questions should be positive. If not, employers should give consideration to the systems and programs that will nurture a "yes" response.

1. Do I know what is expected of me at work?
2. Do I have the materials and equipment I need to do my work right?
3. At work, do I have the opportunity to do what I do best everyday?
4. In the past seven days, have I received recognition or praise for doing good work?
5. Does my supervisor, or someone at work, seem to care about me as a person?
6. Is there someone at work who encourages my development?
7. At work, do my opinions seem to count?

---

[1]Marcus Buckingham and Curt Coffman, *First, Break All the Rules: What the World's Greatest Managers Do Differently* (New York: Simon & Schuster, 1999).

8. Does the mission or purpose of my company make me feel my job is important?
9. Are my coworkers committed to doing quality work?
10. Do I have a best friend at work?
11. In the past six months, has someone at work talked to me about my progress?
12. This past year, have I had opportunities to learn and grow?

To retain employees, you must first recruit them—a topic of growing proportion these days as the war for talent rages on. Again, sadly, professional services firms are not doing the best job they can in this arena. Why? Because firms are generally not asking their leaders to get intimately involved in these activities, and even when they do, the firms are not compensating those leaders who do get involved and who do make a difference.

GET THE RIGHT PEOPLE ON THE BUS

In the bestseller, *Good to Great: Why Some Companies Make the Leap . . . and Others Don't*, Jim Collins discusses the key factors that helped eleven Fortune 500 companies make the transformation from being merely good companies (average in terms of profits and stock performance) to great companies (on average, outperforming the market by seven times over a 15 year period).[2] He and his team of researchers believed they'd find that a brilliant strategy or "superstar CEO" was responsible for the transformation. That's not what they found. In contrast, they found that a critical first step in transforming a company from good to great is "getting the right people on the bus." Great companies put people before strategy.

A large number of the executives in these companies believe that if you have the right people on the bus, you don't need to spend a great deal of time aligning people to strategy or motivating the team—it just happens. On the other hand, if you don't have the right people on the bus, the greatest strategy in the world cannot save you. Notice that the term *compensation* is nowhere to be found in the above paragraph. Generally, however, we think about compensation as a motivator. So, does that mean if we have the right people on the bus and we don't need to spend a great deal of time motivating them, that compensation doesn't matter? Not at all! It means the right compensation system will attract and retain great talent rather than improve mediocre talent.

The Recruiting Process

It's really no secret that we all go to many of the same places to do recruitment—and that we've all thought about the really good ideas for recruitment (for example, campus recruiting, internships, schmoozing college professors, funding scholarships, attending job fairs, working with recruiters, and educating high school students about the profession). So,

---

[2]Jim Collins, *Good to Great: Why Some Companies Make the Leap . . . and Others Don't* (New York: HarperCollins Publishers, 2001).

when it comes to recruitment, let's not focus on who you're going after and how you're going after them (although we don't mean to minimize its importance). You still need to think about who will do the recruiting, how many people from your firm will be involved, which colleges, and who your competitors are, for starters. Let's focus on what you want . . . because the greatest indicator of retention is hiring the right people. So, let's focus on "what" rather than "who."

You really have two choices when interviewing: be interested or be interesting. When in doubt, be interested. Even for areas that are important to share (such as firm history, what you're doing to preserve and improve the firm's reputation, the type of services your firm offers, and the industries on which you focus), ask *them* questions that will lead you to discussions about the things you'd like to share. Most people will only talk in generalities about how they see themselves—so, it is up to you to ask questions that bring out information about their specific experiences. Summarize what you hear and clarify important points, but don't just accept well-rehearsed answers and mere generalities.

Whether you're at a campus recruiting event or in a formal interview at your firm, we cannot overemphasize the importance of the questions you ask. Remember Pareto's Principle: You want them doing 80 percent of the talking. You do that by asking questions, but not just any questions. You need to be asking the types of questions that other firms don't ask. If they do most of the talking and you do most of the listening, you'll have lots of time to form an opinion. And that's the purpose of the interview. And everyone they meet in the recruitment process must be on the same page. Now, of course, there are going to be a variety of technical questions that need to be asked, but it's also important to ask questions that put them at ease while helping you get a sense of their values, their ability to relate to colleagues and clients, their desire for continuous learning, their problem-solving ability, their willingness to go the extra mile, and their ability to think on their feet.

Clearly you want to eliminate questions that can be answered with a yes or no. But also resist the temptation to "fill in the blanks" for the interviewee. After asking the questions, just listen! You may paraphrase or clarify for understanding, but resist the urge to add anything to their responses—in other words, get comfortable with the silence. We've created a large list of questions, many of them behavioral based, and we share some examples here:

1. How did you choose to go into this profession?
2. What did you enjoy *most* about your previous job?
3. What did you enjoy *least* about your previous job?
4. What was your favorite college course and why (if candidate is a college recruit)?
5. For what reasons should we hire you?
6. What would your previous or current supervisor (or one of your professors) say are your three greatest strengths? Three weaknesses?
7. What interests or excites you about working for our firm?
8. Describe the best supervisor relationship you have had. What made it work so well?

9. What are your career goals in 1 to 3 years? 5 to 10 years?
10. How would working for our firm help you to meet those goals?
11. Describe a situation in which you worked well on a team.
12. What motivates you? What is demotivating to you?
13. What are your expectations from the firm?
14. Describe a time you disagreed with someone at work. What were the circumstances and how did you handle it?
15. What is an accomplishment you are proud of and why?
16. What does excellent client service mean to you and how do you exhibit it?

Your process should help you identify and select people with the likelihood of having a strong showing in three categories of criteria: Character, competence, and performance (how both character and competence manifest themselves in production). Whether it's for an intern position, a full-time position, or a position that will start at a future date, make your selection as quickly as possible. Then, let the person know why you've selected him or her and what to expect from this point forward.

There's no doubt about it. Making a hiring decision can be like a roll of the dice. But if you spend adequate time establishing job criteria, preparing for the interview, and developing great interview questions, you'll get great information from candidates. This method may not be infallible, but at least you'll be able to make more informed decisions, increasing the likelihood of getting the right people on the bus and in the right seats.

Five Important Criteria for Getting the Right People on the Bus

Hiring decisions are some of the most important we'll make as leaders in our firms. This is evidenced by the number of leaders who are willing to budget dollars for psychological or behavioral testing and assessment for prospective employees or who are willing to elongate the process to seek second opinions about potential employees.

Regardless of what a great leader others may think you are, you're only as good as your weakest contributor. If you make a poor hiring decision, the impact of that decision can have serious costs throughout the firm. First, there are financial costs—both direct and indirect. Direct costs often include advertising, and time to recruit, interview, orient, and train. Indirect costs may include the loss of clients who were not well served by the new hire.

Then, there are hidden costs—losing mediocre (or even good) employees who simply were not "matches" for our firm's mission, vision, and values; and losing great employees who become disgruntled when mediocre employees are treated in the same manner as great ones. Echoing the theme from Jim Collins that a key strategy for great performance is to "get the right people on the bus," Michael Hudson from Everyday Leadership Network says, "Tolerating a subpar performer brings everyone else in the organization down. Worse than that, it cripples the individual by virtually eliminating any opportunity for growth and advancement."

According to one of Jim Collins' personal messages on the Web site, www.jimcollins.com, the five key criteria for knowing whether you have the right people on the right bus are as follows:

1. The person must already have a predisposition for or share the core values of the firm. If not, reject him or her!
2. It is not someone you need to manage.
3. In key positions, does he or she have exceptional capability? In the seat held, could that person potentially be one of the best in the industry in that particular seat? Doesn't mean he or she is, but it's possible.
4. The person understands the difference between having a job and having a responsibility. He or she worries three steps ahead and is "productively neurotic." If there's a hole to be filled, he or she fills it.
5. Ask yourself, "If it were a hiring decision all over again, given everything we now know, would we still hire him or her?"

The most important thing to keep in mind when evaluating these criteria, however, is to be fair. If there's ever a doubt or if you're wondering about someone, ask whether it's a "best" problem or a "seat" problem.

FINAL THOUGHTS

Leaders should execute on the following key items when it comes to recruitment:

- Front load the people process: Each minute devoted to ensuring you have the right people on the bus will save you many more down the road.
- When evaluating candidates, focus more on character and competence (behavioral factors) than education and experience (unless mandatory for the job). Utilize testing and assessment as appropriate.
- Ask yourself periodically Collins' five questions to determine if you have the right people in the right seats on the bus.

At the end of the day, it's the people that will make a difference and distinguish your firm from the competition. As a result, please be sure to build into your compensation system the appropriate rewards for team members who develop effective recruiting systems, develop the skills and abilities to interview effectively, and who generate great results when it comes to attracting and hiring the *right* people.

9

DESIGNING A NEW COMPENSATION SYSTEM: ATTRACT, REWARD, AND RETAIN TOP PERFORMERS

"While compensation is unlikely to drive performance, inequitable compensation decisions hurt morale and consequently diminish performance."

—James D. Cotterman

In this chapter we explore a process you can use to design the right compensation system for your firm. We provide you with the process rather than the answer because, as we have noted, there is no single best compensation system for every firm. Before we get into the design section of the chapter, we look at some key learnings about owner compensation. The chapter closes with suggestions on rolling out a new compensation plan, incentive plans, and noncash rewards.

KEY LEARNINGS

We review key learnings with the hope it will help you understand and evaluate your own compensation system before attempting to replace it with a new or improved system.

The Search for the Holy Grail

According to legend, people have been searching for the ideal—the Holy Grail, the Fountain of Youth, El Dorado—for ages, with little or no success. As far as we know, public accounting firm owners have also long searched for the perfect compensation system with limited success. While there are no doubt countless reasons for this lack of success, the primary reason is likely that compensation systems involve human beings. We could say there is no perfect compensation system because there are no perfect human beings, but we believe saying so is an oversimplification.

No matter how mechanical, objective, mathematical, or systematic your compensation system, the human element cannot be removed—in either the system's creation or owner reaction to its application. Consider the following scenario.

Mary is an owner in an eight-owner firm. She has been an owner for nine years and is a key rainmaker, but not the highest paid owner. John has been an owner for six years and falls in the middle of the owner compensation distribution. John is an outstanding client service owner, but lacks Mary's rainmaking skills. Both receive significant salary increases (in fact, the two highest increases) for their contributions to the practice. John believes he was justly recognized and compensated, and the increase motivates him. Mary, on the other hand, is somewhat disappointed, and her ego suffers. In her heart she believes she is worth more and wants more.

No compensation system will ever eliminate potentially negative human reaction. The late Don Istvan, one of the best-known consultants to the accounting profession in the 1980s and 1990s, once told us, "A good compensation system will keep most owners happy most of the time." Hence, it is not unusual that most compensation systems produce disappointing feelings for some of the owners and staff members in any given year.

Aligning Rewards and Culture

An important factor that predicts how well a compensation system will work is how well it aligns with the firm's culture. When the system rewards behaviors that are contrary to the firm's core values, it creates a disconnect between what is said to be important and what is rewarded. This often is the start of a dysfunctional firm. For example, a midsized firm has "teamwork" as one of its core values. When it came to compensating owners, however, this value was not recognized. Rather, *individual* behavior and results were most highly rewarded.

Show Me the Money!

We already shared that no margin means no mission, but it may also mean the difference between keeping and losing good people. Usually it is not the system itself that causes the problem(s). It is the money—or lack thereof. Money can cure many evils in a poor or unfair compensation system. And as long as there is enough to keep everyone happy, many problems remain out of sight.

Managing the Outcome

A compensation system is a mechanism for rewarding individuals by distributing money, generally firm profits. If it were that simple, however, there would not be as many emotional issues as there usually are. A good system helps firm leaders manage the gamut of human reactions and feelings that occur when compensation decisions are made. But how often do you really consider the emotional impact of your compensation decisions on the individual? If compensation is supposed to motivate and reward good performance (encourage productive behavior and outcomes), and discourage poor performance (discourage nonproductive behavior and outcomes), then you must ask yourself, "How well are we doing?"

Here is a real-life example to consider.

A large public accounting firm is able to reduce an owner's income by up to 15 percent in any given year for lack of performance. Hence, owners who did not perform the previous year experience a decrease in base compensation. However, firm management did a poor job of explaining these compensation decisions because many of the owners were long-time friends. They simply found it too difficult to have an honest discussion about performance.

The firm's attempt to change behavior by using money as the leverage did not work. Underperforming owners did not understand the message, and they did not know how they could improve. Money alone (or lack of it) is generally not the best or only way to communicate poor performance. You still need to have old-fashioned face-to-face conversations to discuss expectations and help underperforming owners improve.

In "Making Better Compensation Decisions," James Cotterman, a principal at Altman Weil, Inc., and leading compensation consultant to the legal profession, notes, "While compensation is unlikely to drive performance, inequitable compensation decisions hurt morale and consequently diminish performance."[1]

WHAT MAKES A GOOD PLAN

While there is no perfect plan, there are many basic characteristics of a good plan. During the course of our consulting we have noted the following questions must be answered affirmatively to help ensure the firm has a good plan. To how many of them can you answer "yes" when it comes to your current compensation plan?

1. Is the system fair?
2. Is it fairly applied?
3. Have you involved those most affected by the plan?
4. Does everyone understand how it works?
5. Does it promote the most profitable work for the firm?
6. Does it create a one-firm concept rather than silos?
7. Does it encourage the owners to live the firm's core values?
8. Does it encourage everyone to do what's best for the clients?
9. Is there some flexibility to reward exceptional performance?
10. Does it substantially reward performers over nonperformers?
11. Does it reward for current production as well as building future capacity?
12. Is the compensation system tied to the firm's strategic goals?
13. Does the system usually provide for predictability in total compensation year over year?
14. Is the system modified from time to time based on the changing needs of the firm?
15. Will the system keep the firm alive after the retirement of the senior owners?

---

[1]James D. Cotterman, "Making Better Compensation Decisions," Report to Legal Management (Altman Weil, Inc., April 2006).

Every compensation plan should be constructed to help the firm achieve its strategic goals and to attract, reward, and retain the right people. If the plan does not accomplish these two objectives, it needs to be restructured, unless your goal, of course, is to attract and retain average or less-than-average performers. Jim Collins in *Good to Great* writes, "The purpose of a compensation system should not be to get the right behavior from the wrong people, but to get the right people on the bus in the first place and then keep them there."[2]

Public accounting firm compensation plans have changed over the past 20 years or so because the business environment and the workforce have dramatically changed and new technology dominates today's business workflow. And even though compensation plans have changed, and continue to change, they remain as one of the most difficult systems to change in *any* organization, especially accounting firms.

Today's workforce also operates somewhat differently from previous generations. There was a time when the employee and the employer had an unwritten social contract. The employee was loyal to the company and vice versa. Somewhere along the line this social contract was broken. Organizations have less loyalty to employees, and employees are often accused of being loyal only to themselves. If this is true, today's workforce needs a different kind of compensation program.

In *Practice What You Preach*, David Maister observed, "The *method* of compensation is largely irrelevant as a causal factor for high and sustained performance." He continues to note, "Those who contributed the most to the overall success of the office are the most highly rewarded. Notice that this does not suggest what the pay scheme should be. The determining factor is just whether the people think it rewards the right people."[3]

Some of the best practices in designing a compensation system include:

■ Embrace a total compensation philosophy which reminds employees that their compensation includes a lot more than just base pay.
■ Define and communicate your compensation philosophy. A focused compensation philosophy answers these fundamental questions:
—What do you want to pay for?
—How do you want to pay for it?
—What is your competitive posture?
—How will you split up the pie?
■ Tailor the plan to your firm's culture and values. Too many professional services firms and corporations generally have little or no connection between their stated values and what the compensation plan rewards. Matching organizational values to performance requires a new approach to compensation.
■ Link compensation to achieving the firm's vision, mission, and strategy. This involves identifying the firm's top strategic objectives,

---

[2]Jim Collins, *Good to Great: Why Some Companies Make the Leap . . . and Others Don't* (New York: Harper Collins Publishers, Inc., 2001), p. 49.
[3]David Maister, *Practice What You Preach* (New York: The Free Press, Simon & Schuster, 2001).

defining what they mean in terms of organizational behavior, and designing your compensation plan in a way that rewards and recognizes those behaviors.

■ Know what creates value in your firm. In accounting firms, value gets created by identifying and satisfying client needs in a profitable manner and by developing processes and systems that improve work flow efficiencies.

■ Create and hold people accountable to competency maps that outline needed skills and behaviors.

■ Focus on criteria that improve both top line and bottom line.

■ Reward skills and behaviors that drive results (for example, developing more efficient processes, training others, billing in a timely fashion). You can only create permanent behavior change by first changing the culture and the environment, then using compensation to reinforce those changes.

■ Measure and reward individual, team, departmental, and firmwide objectives.

DESIGNING A COMPENSATION PLAN

After you address these issues, you can begin to build the actual compensation plan. Remember, many of today's workers are often loyal to themselves first and the firm second. Your father's compensation plan won't work today. Today's workforce requires a very different kind of compensation plan. And while firms will design different plans, there are fundamental and foundational principles to which every plan should align. To ensure adherence to the principles of good design, consider the following 12 items.

1. *Ask foundational questions.* Before getting too far into the design, ask the following questions:
   ■ What is the life of the plan?
   ■ Who will be responsible for administering it?
   ■ Who will participate in the plan? Just owners, or owners and employees?
   ■ How often and when will payments be made?
   ■ How will you determine the payout?
   ■ How will you measure the goal?
   ■ How will you track results?
   ■ Will there be minimum thresholds or will it be an all-or-nothing payout?

2. *Ensure the plan is win-win-win.* For any compensation plan to succeed over time, it must meet the needs of three critical stakeholders: clients, employees, and other stakeholders. Secondary stakeholders include employees' family members, vendors and suppliers, referral sources, the community, and so on.

3. *Use both satisfiers and motivators.* In the mid 1960s management theorist Frederick Herzberg made a discovery that changed the way in which people understood motivation in the workplace. Herzberg

interviewed 200 engineers and accountants and asked them about one positive and one negative work experience they had encountered. He then probed their answers to find out what was behind each experience. Herzberg discovered a group of "satisfiers" that were generally responsible for positive experiences, and a set of "dissatisfiers" that were generally responsible for negative workplace experiences. Satisfiers (base pay, benefits, and so on) allow you to attract and retain people but don't motivate performance. Motivators (pay-for-performance incentives, empowerment, recognition, job opportunities, growth and learning, and so on) drive people to improve performance.

4. *Get owners, employees, or both involved in the design.* We like to say, "No involvement, no commitment." Be sure you provide all owners an opportunity to participate in the design of the plan. By inviting participation, valuing all viewpoints, and brainstorming about the whys and hows, it is more than possible to design a system that is both fair and objective.

5. *Balance rewards for results and effort.* While you always want to pay for results, it is also important to recognize effort. Owners who worked hard for results but failed to achieve them based on circumstances outside their control should receive recognition, even if it is not monetary.

6. *Identify measures, define targets, and track performance.* Measures need to be identified. For example, a measure could be "new business development." A target for an owner could be three to five new clients with total revenue of $50,000 to $75,000. Then achievement toward the target is tracked and reported monthly.

7. *Strive to create high trust within the firm.* Low trust can kill a compensation plan, and changing compensation plans in a negative or low-trust environment is virtually impossible. The best way to raise trust in an organization, and therefore make needed changes to compensation, is to build personal character and competence within individuals so they can create trusting relationships with each other. Not only must individuals talk the talk, they must walk the walk. This is a case where actions speak louder than words.

8. *Avoid side or one-off agreements.* When recognizing and rewarding superior performance, do not have special agreements; they can create different classes of citizens in your firm. Every employee within a specific role should have the same bonus opportunity or potential for similar performance. Superstars generally work well under such a system. Remember, however, one great year does not make a superstar. Over time, a real superstar's base compensation generally increases substantially over the average performer. In addition, the superstar should receive annual bonus payments far above the average performer.

9. *Communicate, communicate, communicate.* Implementing a new or revised compensation plan requires constant and detailed communication. Ensure you allocate sufficient time to involve everyone in the design of the program, explain the program, answer questions about the program, and allow individuals to see how they would have been affected by it had your firm been "on this plan" last year.

10. *Reengage.* During the first year, it is necessary to recommit and reengage everyone often. If there are problems with the initial design, acknowledge them and make needed modifications.

11. *Budget for bonuses.* There is nothing as disappointing as working hard to achieve goals, meeting the goals, and receiving absolutely no bonus for your efforts. On the flip side, it is difficult for the firm to distribute significant bonus dollars when it has not reached its desired profitability goals. We therefore suggest a modest budget to ensure deserving individuals receive bonuses and deserving individuals receive *significant* bonuses only to the degree the firm reaches its goals. If all owners and staff in a firm achieve their goals, the financial results generally fall and paying bonuses is not problematic.

12. *Pay for performance.* Make sure you separate base compensation from incentive pay. Focus your plan on rewarding and paying for performance, results, and productivity.

ROLLING OUT THE PLAN

Perhaps the best way to implement a new compensation plan is to run the old and new plans simultaneously for a year. You pay based on the old plan, but show employees what they would have earned under the new plan. By using this method you can ensure:

- The new plan creates alignment.
- You are able to track measures and provide periodic reports.
- Communication is timely and on target.
- You are able to debug any problems.

Once you unveil the plan, meet regularly and often with employees and owners to make sure people understand the plan as well as the actions they must take to meet the stated goals. As you gain experience with the new plan, ask yourself the following questions:

- Are we seeing the right behaviors from employees and owners?
- Is overall productivity improving?
- Is owner and employee morale improving?
- Are we on track to achieve our goals?
- Are we gaining alignment with key stakeholders—employees, clients, and owners?

INCENTIVE PLAN SUCCESS FACTORS

A recent survey by Meek & Associates, Strategic Compensation Consultants, asked 312 companies about their use of incentives and bonuses. The four most successful incentive plan practices, as reported by these TEC, Inc., members, were:

- Linking incentives to the company's business results
- Tying the plan to performance (quantitative and qualitative)
- Communicating as much and as frequently as possible
- Involving employees in the process

The four biggest mistakes in incentive plan design and implementation were:

- Insufficient communication and feedback
- Lack of alignment with the business strategy and objectives
- Using discretionary measures
- Setting unrealistic goals

When asked what they would do differently the next time around, TEC, Inc., members responded most often with:

- Tie incentives to results and performance
- Communicate, communicate, communicate
- Pay out more frequently
- Share financial and business information[4]

INCLUDE NONCASH REWARDS

While cash will always be king, you should also provide your people with noncash rewards and recognition. These are important elements of your overall compensation program. The best way to find out what is important to your people is simply to ask them. This can be done through surveys, focus group meetings, individual interviews, or a combination of these methods.

You will find a wide range of ideas and wants. The best approach is to offer a number of choices rather than just one or two. Examples follow.

- Many firms hold a monthly reward ceremony. The important thing about this event is not so much the actual rewards given, but the individual recognition. Make sure you take time to tell a story about why employees receive these rewards. The more personal you can make it the better.
- Employees should be able to recognize and reward each other as well as owners. This is especially critical when trying to change firm culture. You want employees and owners to acknowledge others, especially those who exemplify your core values.
- Consider changing the noncash rewards every year. Always getting the same reward does not create new excitement. You may also want to consider different reward tiers.
- Finally, there are two words not heard often enough in accounting firms: thank you. You can get a lot of mileage from merely saying "thank you" when people do a good job.

---

[4]Source: http://www.teconline.com/www/bestpractices/compensation.asp.

FINAL THOUGHTS

In "Follow the Money—the Evolution of Owner Compensation Systems in Law Firms," Blane R. Prescott, a Hildebrandt International consultant, noted, "Almost all systems produce disappointing results at some time, so most firms are always on the lookout for ways to improve the process, to discover another system that is better or easier, or one which prompts fewer negative reactions among owners. The desire for a better system is therefore both natural and understandable, yet many firms would be well served to understand this simple rule of thumb: *There is no such thing as a perfect owner compensation system, and just because the one being used occasionally fails, it may be closer to perfect than one might realize.*"[5]

---

[5]Blane R. Prescott, "Follow the Money—The Evolution of Partner Compensation Systems in Law Firms" (Hildebrandt, December 21, 1999).

10

SETTING GOALS AND MANAGING PERFORMANCE

"The reason most people never reach their goals is that they don't define them, or ever seriously consider them as believable or achievable. Winners can tell you where they are going, what they plan to do along the way, and who will be sharing the adventure with them."

—Denis Waitley

When owners or employees express concern with their compensation systems, many people argue it is a result of a flawed compensation system. We argue that in addition to the possibility of a faulty system, one of two things is likely happening: either individuals do not understand the compensation system, or firm leaders do not manage performance. Employees need a goal-setting process that creates a "line of sight"—they need to be able to draw a line of sight between the firm's vision and strategic objectives and what they do on a daily basis, and they need to understand how what they do on a daily basis translates to compensation. They also need frequent, accurate, and specific feedback to let them know how they are performing. Firms often have these systems—but all too often *these* are the systems that are flawed, either in their design or their execution.

This chapter covers the basics of goal setting and a process you can use to set and monitor progress toward goal achievement. We realize there is more than one way to set and monitor goals. The process itself is not as important as the consistency with which it is followed—for both goal setting and goal monitoring. Again, it is the consistent application of the process that counts.

"LINE OF SIGHT" OR CASCADING PERFORMANCE GOALS

A performance goal (often referred to as a performance target) is an explicit statement of what a firm or individual will accomplish during the current year or performance cycle. Individual goals are based on the firm's overall goals, departmental goals, and team goals. Goals generally depend on the employee's level and role in the firm. It is best to set and monitor individual performance goals based on firm-wide goals that are cascaded throughout the organization. These are merely high-level goals that are set by the firm, and every employee participates in achieving them. This is where the concept of "line of sight" comes into play.

Individual performance goals should be based, or closely aligned to, the goals of those above them in the firm. For example, a manager's goals should support the goals of one or more owner's goals. The owner's goals should support the goals of the department in which he or she works which, in turn, should support the goals of the firm. In many firms, the rainmaker is highly compensated, but the business that he or she brings into the firm may not be tied to the firm's strategic vision. If so, rewarding such performance is probably counterproductive.

To help employees increase "line of sight," you may want to flowchart how their activities support the goals of their superiors and how their superiors' goals support the goals above them.

The Ritz-Carlton often serves as one of the best examples of how corporate goals are cascaded throughout an organization. See Exhibit 10–1, "The Ritz-Carlton's Gold Standards," at the end of the chapter.

Cascading goals for a typical accounting firm are illustrated in the following figure.

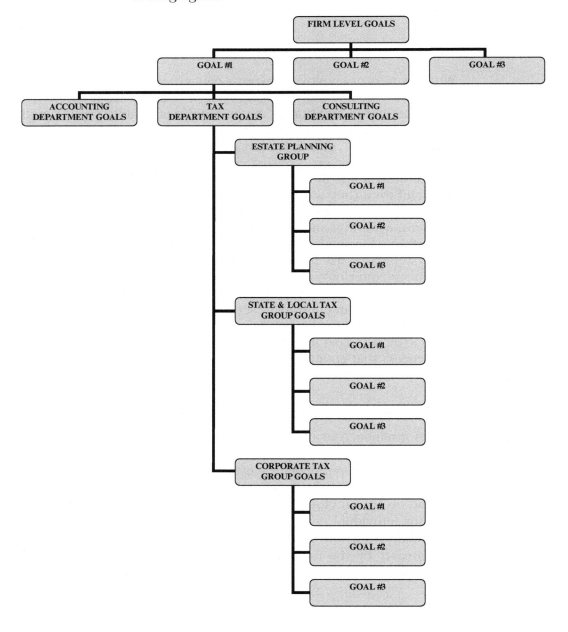

SET CASCADING PERFORMANCE GOALS

"In most cases, goals that do exist are vastly undercommunicated," says Stephen R. Covey. "Just because the formal leaders are clear on what they want to achieve doesn't necessarily mean that those on the front line, where the action actually happens, know what the goals are."[1]

At the beginning of each fiscal year, each employee, together with his or her manager or owner, should develop agreed-upon individual performance goals that align with the firm's strategic goals—using some type of goal-setting form or template. Not only are goals defined at the beginning of the year, but measures and targets for success for each goal are also defined. At the end of the year, these measures are used to determine the degree to which the employee or owner has achieved each goal.

Some firms use a numerical rating which is applied to each goal category based on how well the employee has achieved the goals in that category. One example of such a rating scale is:

1 = Far exceeds expectations
2 = Exceeds expectations
3 = Meets expectations
4 = Below expectations
5 = Far below expectations

Leader Responsibilities in Setting Cascading Performance Goals

Leaders have the following responsibilities for helping employees set performance goals. Leaders should:

- Provide appropriate employees with a copy of the firm's strategic performance goals, his or her departmental performance goals, and the leader's individual goals.
- Meet with employees to discuss how they can help the firm achieve its strategic goals (that is, create a "line of sight"). This meeting should occur before employees begin the process of writing their goals.
- Provide assistance, as necessary, to ensure the goals employees create follow the SMART (specific, measurable, achievable, relevant, and time-bound) format and align with firm goals.
- Review and approve, as appropriate, the goals each employee writes—ensuring the goals are a win for both the employee and the firm.
- Ensure each employee develops and implements a professional development plan that supports goal achievement.
- Hold employees accountable for achieving their goals.
- Offer resources, feedback, coaching, and support employees' needs to achieve their goals.
- Meet regularly (at least quarterly) with employees to discuss progress toward goal achievement and revise them as appropriate.
- Conduct a formal assessment of each employee's progress toward goal achievement at midyear.
- Conduct a formal assessment of each employee's goal achievement at year-end.

---

[1]Stephen R. Covey, during 7 Habits Certification Class, March 2005, in Homestead, Utah.

Employee Responsibilities Setting Cascading Performance Goals

Employees have the following responsibilities for goal setting. Employees should:

- Review the firm's strategic performance goals, their departmental performance goals, and their leader's individual goals.
- Ask their leaders how they can help the firm achieve its strategic goals (that is, create a "line of sight").
- Write a first draft of their goals and ensure the performance goals follow the SMART (specific, measurable, achievable, relevant, and time-bound) format.
- Meet with their leaders to discuss and refine the performance goals to ensure they align with the firm's goals.
- Develop and implement a professional development plan that supports goal achievement.
- Work hard to accomplish their performance goals and be accountable for achieving them.
- Seek the resources, feedback, coaching, and support they need to achieve their goals.
- Meet regularly (at least quarterly) with their leaders to discuss progress toward goal achievement and revise them as appropriate.
- Document progress toward achievement of their performance goals so they can discuss progress as well as needed adjustments with their leaders during a formal, midyear assessment.
- Document progress toward achievement of their performance goals so they can discuss goal accomplishment (or lack thereof) with their leaders during a formal, year-end assessment.

A caveat: As one managing owner told us, "I wholeheartedly agree and support all of this—and we do it and it works—*however*, it takes a *lot* of time and effort and few firms will sacrifice the billable time it takes (away from the firm) to get this done." While it does take time, we believe the rewards for both individuals and the firm are well worth the effort.

PREPARE TO WRITE CASCADING PERFORMANCE GOALS

"U.S. workers have so many goals to work on, they can't stay focused on and execute their organization's top three goals," says Stephen R. Covey in *The 8th Habit.* "They need clear direction from senior level management, as well as their direct supervisors, in distinguishing the difference between goals which are merely important and those which are wildly important—those which must be reached or nothing else matters."[2]

We shared previously that leaders are responsible for providing employees with copies of the leaders' goals, the department's goals, and the firm's strategic goals and objectives. Employees should review their leaders' goals to understand how the goals have cascaded from the top of the organization to their leaders.

---

[2]Stephen R. Covey, *The 8th Habit: From Effectiveness to Greatness* (New York: Free Press, 2004).

Employees and their leaders should discuss how employees can help accomplish the firm's strategic goals and objectives as well as the leader's goals. Employees may be asked to be responsible entirely for accomplishing one or more of the goals, or they may be asked to be accountable for only certain tasks within specific goals. When meeting, everyone should:

- Understand desired outcomes.
- Consider other factors (for example, culture, firm policies, possible barriers, and so on).
- Remain aware of the resources (people, financial, technological, training, and so on) available to help accomplish the performance goals.
- Agree about how progress (that is, accountability) will be monitored.
- Understand the consequences of accomplishing (or not accomplishing) the goal(s).

You may also need to talk with key internal customers or stakeholders. Their needs help you define your goals. Before creating goals, take the following three steps:

1. Be sure you know specifically what you are trying to accomplish.
2. Focus on outcomes, not activities.
3. Write clear and explicit statements of what you will achieve.

WRITE CASCADING PERFORMANCE GOALS

As it is written, so it shall happen. In *What They Don't Teach You at Harvard Business School*, author Mark McCormack found that only 3 percent of the 1979 Harvard Business School class had written down their goals and plans. Ten years after graduation, that 3 percent earned an average of 10 times more money than the rest of their classmates. What is the moral of the story? Write your goals! At the same time, we recommend you limit the number of written performance goals. According to FranklinCovey's execution process, *The 4 Disciplines of Execution*™ (a work session that helps managers and teams identify their highest priorities), the traditional thinking suggested that workers can effectively accomplish six, eight, or even ten important goals at once. The new thinking suggests that workers who narrow their focus on a few key goals have a greater chance of achieving their goals with excellence. Too many goals, conflicting or not, lead to confusion, burnout, decline in quality, and loss of focus. Goals must be specific and clear, explicitly linked to corporate strategy, broken down into bite-size chunks, measurable, and deadline-driven.

As goals are completed throughout the year, new goals may be added. If you have a large number of goals (more than five), it is likely that what you are calling goals are actually tasks or parts of larger goals. Remember, a goal should be based on a major area of responsibility.

Many people use the SMART acronym as a reminder about how to write effective performance goals (targets). Again, a SMART goal is specific, measurable, achievable, relevant, and time-bound. A SMART goal states the expected outcomes as simply and concretely as possible. It answers questions such as: "By how much?", "For whom?", and "For what?"

Here is an exercise to help you write goals that are focused on outcomes rather than activities. It helps you increase clarity and specificity about the important outcomes. For each goal, ask yourself the question, "How will I or anyone else recognize success?" Write down your answer. Then modify the question based on your previous answer. Repeat the process until you have a specific outcome-based goal. If, for example, your goal is to increase service to tax clients, you may ask the following:

Q: How will I and others recognize success in service to tax clients?
A: By returning work to them prior to an agreed-upon deadline.
Q: How will I and others recognize that work was returned prior to an agreed-upon deadline?
A: By tracking when the work was sent vs. when the work was promised to be sent.
Q: How will I and others recognize success in sent vs. promised work?
A: By improving my "sent prior to the deadline" rate from 72% to 95%.

To commit ourselves to our goals, we must first identify with them. We *want* to achieve them, we *need* to achieve them. Most people want goals that increase their learning and challenge them to go beyond former achievements. When you write your goals, think about how you can make an impact. Think about how to tackle new problems or address familiar issues in creative ways. If you write challenging (but achievable) goals, your work will be more interesting and fulfilling, and your contribution to the firm will be larger.

In some performance management goal forms there can be a space for you to indicate the primary beneficiary or the upper-level goal your goal supports. For example, an administrative assistant might have an internal client goal to "provide efficient administrative support to the Audit Department." The primary beneficiaries would be the members of the department. An audit manager's client goal might read, "Help reduce staff turnover from 10 percent to 5 percent by December 31 of next year." In this case, primary beneficiaries may include both clients and other staff members.

Almost everyone needs to work cooperatively with others in the firm to achieve their goals. To create further "line of sight," document the names of the people or groups with whom you will work to accomplish your goals. These individuals or groups may be internal or external clients, colleagues, managers, or owners.

DEFINE MEASURES OF SUCCESS FOR CASCADING PERFORMANCE GOALS

In FranklinCovey's *4 Disciplines of Execution*™, we are reminded that traditional thinking suggests that once the goal has been communicated, workers will know the organization is serious about it. In reality, workers are not really serious about a goal until they start keeping score.

A measure of success is a verifiable indicator of results. It is the target. It is how the achievement of your goals will be measured. "Verifiable" here means that other people would agree, on the basis of the measure you specify, that the desired results were achieved or not achieved. For each goal, write one to three measures of success. Year-end goal ratings will be based upon these measures of success. The measures must focus on observable results, that is, your leader and others must be able to verify that you have accomplished your goal.

We learn in *The 4 Disciplines of Execution*™ that creating measures and a compelling scoreboard that is accessible, visual, engaging, attainable, and concise ensures workers have the same understanding of goals and can see when they are winning or when course correction must be made.

CATEGORIES OF CASCADING GOAL MEASURES

While goal categories (and their weighting) vary from firm to firm, we believe each firm should have, at a minimum, the following basic goal categories (which tie to the categories in the Balanced Scorecard):

1. Financial goals
2. Client goals
3. Internal systems/business process goals
4. Employee growth and learning goals
5. Business development goals

How these categories are weighted for the computation of year-end performance ratings varies from firm to firm and often varies from person to person within a particular firm. Each is discussed in the following sections.

Financial Measures[3]

The proof, as they say, is in the pudding. The financial perspective tells a firm if its strategies are working. If the firm is hitting or exceeding its growth and profitability goals, then it is effectively implementing its strategic plan. If financial measures are not being accomplished, the firm is compelled to examine underperforming areas and make needed changes to get better results. While most firms are good at setting financial objectives, neglecting what is behind the numbers often gets them into trouble. The most common measures in the financial area include:

■ Staff cost as a percent of net revenue
■ Revenue from new services introduced
■ Revenue growth

---

[3]Much of this section comes from *Client at the Core: Marketing and Managing Today's Professional Services Firm*, by August Aquila and Bruce W. Marcus (Hoboken, N.J.: John Wiley & Sons, 2004), Appendix A, pp 247-255. Reprinted with permission of John Wiley & Sons, Inc.

- Net income per partner/owner (NIPP)
- Return on investment (ROI)
- Return on marketing investment (ROMI)
- Operating margin
- Market share
- Return on equity (ROE: earnings available to shareholders/shareholders' equity)
- Profits per professional
- Profits per full-time equivalent (FTE)
- Revenue by service mix
- Cash flow from operations
- Receivables as a percent of working capital
- Days outstanding in accounts receivable (A/R) and work in process (WIP)

Client Measures

Client objectives tell you how well you are servicing the market segments in which you have chosen to compete. To determine how well they are achieving the firm's client objectives, firms often select one or more measures from the following list:

- Number of personal interviews with clients
- Client service guarantees implemented
- Profitability by client
- Number of clients inside the target market segment
- Number of profitable clients
- Share of client's wallet
- Accounts receivable (A/R) adjustments
- Work in process (WIP) adjustments
- Client retention rates
- Satisfaction scores in problem areas
- Service attributes
- Percent of clients that rate the firm as 4 or 5 (on a scale from 1 to 5) in client service
- Retention rates or percentage of clients who are repeat
- Number of client complaints
- Number of re-dos in work products (error rate)
- Number of clients exercising service guarantee
- Number of new services sold to existing clients
- Service quality
- Turnaround time
- Percent of delivery deadlines met
- Percentage of total revenue that comes from repeat clients
- Percentage of lost clients
- Net clients gained
- Percent of clients providing referrals

Internal Systems/Business Process Measures

Many business leaders believe a great strategy is the key to getting desired business results. One statement that has had a profound impact on us as consultants is this: "A Grade C strategy with Grade A execution is far better than a Grade A strategy with Grade C execution." As we saw in the Organizational Effectiveness Cycle in Chapter 3, "systems and process" are what follow closely on the heels of strategy. It is the systems and processes that cause or motivate people to engage (or not to engage) in the behaviors that are needed to accomplish the goals.

While some accounting firms, and many consulting firms, provide process reengineering for their clients, few do so within their own firms. Simply stated, a process is a series of steps that change input into output. There are many processes in a firm, but the most important ones are those that have an impact on the client's experience with the firm and on the firm's financial results. The ultimate objective in every business process is to help the firm achieve its goals. Most firms have a goal to provide excellent client service (effective and efficient service). If the work review (quality control) process is redundant and ineffective, however, it is more difficult for the firm to achieve the client service goal.

Process improvement requires a firm to identify, document, and ultimately refine the process so it furthers firm goals. It is an ongoing endeavor.

We encourage firms to assign individual stewardship for existing systems and process review and refinement. These stewardships should be documented as written performance goals for those to whom they are assigned. When assigning process review and refinement, you should outline desired results and allow the stewards to determine the approach and methodology for conducting the reviews and revisions.

When documenting existing systems and processes, we often suggest a flowchart of the tasks and activities that are included in the process as well as decision-points along the way—those steps that convert the input into an output. A flowchart can also demonstrate how the system is currently working. Since processes support many different functions, departments, niches, services, or strategies in a firm, you will want the flowchart to depict all the cross-functional responsibilities. Creating effective internal processes is also important because it reduces inefficiencies, thus allowing more time for professional staff members to work on challenging and motivating client work.

When setting process improvement objectives that impact clients, consider the following broad questions:

- How does the firm need to be structured to meet client needs?
- How does the firm ensure a quality product that eliminates re-dos?
- How does the firm ensure a timely turnaround?
- What does the firm need to do from a process perspective to achieve its client and financial objectives?
- What processes does the firm need to develop or improve in the service innovation, operations, and post-sale stages?

Here are examples of key internal systems and business processes you may want to examine:

- Marketing and sales
- Client acquisition
- Service delivery
- New service development (R&D)
- Post-sales follow-up
- Client service (handling complaints, billing issues)
- Pricing
- Client billing and collection
- Improving utilization
- Turnaround time for projects
- Rework time
- Number of tax returns completed per day
- Number of new services developed
- Time to bring new services to market

Employee Growth and Learning Measures

The employee perspective in a professional services firm is perhaps the most important category of measures because the key differentiating factor for professional services firms is their people—the resources who actually develop and maintain client relationships and provide product or service delivery. The professional services firm succeeds or fails in the other categories (client service, financial, internal systems and business processes, and business development) based on the experience and expertise of its employees.

Employee measures help the firm determine how well it is recruiting and retaining the "right" people and enhancing the competencies of employees and owners. Here are examples of specific measures that determine how well you are achieving employee-related objectives.

- Number of professionals who are trained in more than one service area
- Number of professionals trained in new technologies
- Firm's investment in technology as a percent of net revenue
- Employee satisfaction
- Number of staff suggestions made
- Number of staff suggestions implemented
- Employee turnover ratio
- Average length of service for professionals
- Number of employees participating in retirement and profit-sharing plans
- Revenue generated per employee
- Percentage of professionals with CPA or other professional designation
- Number of professional, niche, and community organizations in which the individual actively participates

Business Development Measures

It should be recognized while an entire firm can sometimes—but not often—be marketed as a firm (for example, "The Firm of Smith and Dale Does Nice Work"), the most effective professional services marketing and business development is performed for the parts of a firm. The performance goals and measures of every niche, practice group, or service team should support the firm's overall strategies.

There are several ways to measure whether your marketing and business development efforts support your firm's growth and financial objectives. For example, you can measure:

- Number of new products or niches developed during the last year
- Number of new geographic markets entered
- Number of cross-selling opportunities created
- Amount of cross-sold revenue
- Cost of new client acquisition
- Number of personal interviews with clients
- Results of client satisfaction surveys
- Number of client service guarantees implemented
- Client profitability
- Number of clients inside the target market segment
- Share of client's wallet
- Client retention rates
- Total marketing cost as a percentage of total revenue
- Number of seminars presented
- Number of ads placed
- Number of interviews conducted
- Number of articles placed
- Number of press releases placed
- Number of times firm members are quoted or mentioned in publications
- Number of presentations made
- Ratio of proposals won/total proposals
- Number of pending proposals
- Number of trade shows attended
- Number of trade shows exhibited at
- Market share
- Number of new clients
- Brand name awareness
- Average fees per existing client
- Average fees per new client
- Percent of sales from new services
- Revenue growth rate by service

SET TASKS AND ACTION STEPS

After you identify your performance goals (targets) and measures, you need to list the tasks you will complete to accomplish the goals. Most people consider tasks to be small. In this context, tasks should not be considered to be the elements of a detailed project plan but rather a list of major milestones. Each of the milestones can be broken down into several steps.

For example, you may establish a goal to "reduce the attrition of five- to seven-year professionals from 15 percent to 10 percent by December 31, 20XX." This goal could be broken down as follows:

- *Goal:* Reduce the attrition of five- to seven-year professionals from 15 percent to 10 percent by 12/31/20XX.
- *Task:* Analyze the reasons for attrition.
  —*Action Step:* Create "attrition task force."
  —*Action Step:* Assign leader of "attrition task force."
  —*Action Step:* Convene first meeting of "attrition task force."
  —*Action Step:* Create agenda for first meeting of "attrition task force."
  —*Action Step:* Plan the analysis methodology.
  —*Action Step:* Conduct focus group interviews.
  —*Action Step:* Perform employee satisfaction survey.
- *Task:* Create a pilot program to boost retention.
- *Task:* Develop and implement a long-term strategy to increase retention and tenure in position.

DETERMINE PERSONAL READINESS LEVEL

For each task, individuals must determine their readiness level for completing the task. This links back to our discussion about *know-what, know-how,* and *know-why.* Readiness level is based on an understanding of what to do, how to do it, and the motivation to do it. You may have a high level of readiness for one task and a low level of readiness for another task within the same goal. You will generally find yourself at one of the following four levels of readiness:

Level 1. You have not yet developed the competencies needed to complete the task, and you have limited self-confidence or motivation. This is called "low skill, low will."

Level 2. You have not yet developed the competencies needed to complete the task, but you have self-confidence and motivation. This is called "low skill, high will."

Level 3. You have the competencies needed to complete the task but you have limited self-confidence or motivation. This is called "high skill, low will."

Level 4. You have both the competencies needed to complete the task and self-confidence and motivation. This is called "high skill, high will."

It is important to determine readiness level because it helps determine the amount and type of support needed to complete the task. To determine the amount and type of leadership needed to complete your tasks based on readiness level, some firms use a "situational leadership" approach. Each of the four types of situational leadership (directing, guiding, supporting, and delegating) corresponds to one of the four categories of readiness.

For individuals at readiness level 1 (low skill, low will) leaders should use a *directing* leadership style. They should provide clear and specific direction, guidelines and rules, training as needed, and close super-vision with frequent review meetings (including coaching and feedback).

For individuals at readiness level 2 (low skill, high will) for a task, lead-ers should use a *guiding* leadership style. They should provide clear but general direction, needed training, and frequent review meetings (includ-ing coaching and feedback). Leaders should involve the task steward in planning the work.

For individuals at readiness level 3 (high skill, low will), leaders should use a *supporting* leadership style. They should ask for and listen to con-cerns about performing the task and encourage the task steward to take action. Leaders should periodically check on progress and provide coach-ing and feedback.

Finally, for individuals at readiness level 4 (high skill, high will), lead-ers should use a *delegating* leadership style. This allows the task steward to take charge of the task and handle as much responsibility as possible. Leaders should take prudent risks in letting task stewards make decisions, but they should also check on progress periodically and provide coaching and feedback.

PREPARE FINAL CASCADING PERFORMANCE GOALS

After you prepare a final draft of your performance goals, meet with your leader to review them. (In the case of owners, they may meet with a man-aging partner or executive committee.) In addition to reviewing each goal, you and your leader should agree on your readiness level for the required tasks as well as any support you may need (for example, training to improve competencies). This should be documented and in your personal and professional development plan.

After meeting with your leader and agreeing on your performance goals for the year, you will document them on the goal form, and each of you should "sign off" on them. Each of you should keep a copy. A sample form is included in Exhibit 10–2, "Sample Form: Setting Performance Goals."

MANAGE PERFORMANCE

Many leaders believe people will remain focused and committed to their performance goals if the goals are clear and compelling. Again, according to FranklinCovey's *4 Disciplines of Execution*™, frequent team engage-ment and accountability is necessary to maintain commitment to goals. Managing performance, therefore, is not something that is done only at year end. Workers must know they are being held accountable, and they must hold each other accountable for their performance.

Bruce Tulgan, author of *FAST Feedback*, suggests the difference between a low-performing team and a high-performing team lies in a coaching-style manager who knows how to keep individual performers focused and motivated day after day. In our work with clients, we often recommend the following agenda items for a team meeting:

■ Celebrate successes
■ Discuss what we learned since the last meeting and how it applies in our work with clients
■ Review firm, department, niche, and team performance goals and progress toward goal achievement
■ Review individual task stewardships since the last team meeting to determine if they have been completed
■ Discuss upcoming individual task stewardships to determine barriers that need to be removed and resources or assistance that may be needed

In addition to regular team meetings, individual performance reviews (feedback sessions) should be conducted to track accountability and discuss progress toward individual performance goals. Tulgan believes employees should receive FAST feedback. Tulgan's acronym, FAST, stands for *frequent, accurate, specific,* and *timely*—the four qualities that employees most often ascribe to feedback from "the best manager they ever had" and feedback they need but do not get from most managers. Employees should receive both positive and constructive feedback.

Frequent. We believe individual performance reviews (feedback sessions) should be conducted at least quarterly.

Accurate. Throughout the year, all employees and owners need to document task completion and goal accomplishment. As tasks are completed, they should be tracked on the goal sheet so progress can be tracked. In addition to your tracking, your leader may use his or her own documentation, feedback from others, and his or her observations to rate your performance. Tracking progress throughout the year about what has already happened alleviates the midyear and year-end scramble to pull it all together for the formal review. Progress is already neatly documented, requiring the addition of only a few notes prior to the formal review.

Specific. While accurate feedback focuses on what has *already* happened, specific feedback focuses on what *needs* to happen. Specific feedback helps employees determine the specific behaviors needed to achieve their "line of sight" or cascading performance goals. In some cases, goals may need to be updated. You may also determine that additional tasks are necessary to complete a certain goal or previously identified tasks are no longer necessary to complete a certain goal. Some goals may no longer be necessary in light of strategic changes at the departmental or firm level. Finally, some goals may have been completed, allowing for the addition of new goals. As goals are updated, we suggest you keep copies of the outdated goal sheets.

Timely. Tulgan and countless others believe the sooner feedback follows the performance in question, the more impact the feedback has on the employee, and the better the chances that any needed improvements will be made.

FINAL THOUGHTS

When changes are contemplated in a firm's goal setting, performance management, and compensation systems, the first question most people ask is, "How will this affect me?" It must be more than merely completing forms, meeting with employees three or four times per year to track accomplishment, and paying for a job well done. We agree with Jim Collins that a performance management system tailored to your firm can attract and retain the "right" people. We like to think that a performance management system does not necessarily create a "survival of the fittest" environment, but rather a "survival of the right people" environment.

While managing performance is not always easy, it is vitally important for the long-term success of the firm. And without undying commitment by owners, performance management will be inconsistent, or, worse yet, nonexistent. We therefore often suggest that owners serve as the role model or example—that they agree to needed changes in their own goal setting, performance management, and compensation systems first—because the best way to influence positive change is to *be* the change we seek.

EXHIBIT 10–1   The Ritz-Carlton's Gold Standards*

The Gold Standards (as posted on The Ritz-Carlton Web site, www.ritzcarlton. com) are the foundation of The Ritz-Carlton Hotel Company, L.L.C. They encompass the values and philosophy by which the hotel operates and include the following (with our bracketed comments in italic).

THE CREDO

The Ritz-Carlton is a place where the genuine care and comfort of our guests is our highest mission. We pledge to provide the finest personal service and facilities for our guests who will always enjoy a warm, relaxed, yet refined ambience.

The Ritz-Carlton experience enlivens the senses, instills well-being, and fulfills even the unexpressed wishes and needs of our guests.

THE MOTTO

At The Ritz-Carlton Hotel Company, L.L.C., "We are ladies and gentlemen serving ladies and gentlemen." This motto exemplifies the anticipatory service provided by all staff members.

THE THREE STEPS OF SERVICE

1. A warm and sincere greeting. Use the guest's name.
2. Anticipation and fulfillment of each guest's needs.
3. Fond farewell. Give a warm good-bye and use the guest's name.

[*There is no confusion about how service should show up in behavior.*]

SERVICE VALUES

1. I build strong relationships and create Ritz-Carlton guests for life.
2. I am always responsive to the expressed and unexpressed wishes and needs of our guests.
3. I am empowered to create unique, memorable and personal experiences for our guests.
4. I understand my role in achieving the Key Success Factors and creating The Ritz-Carlton Mystique.
5. I continuously seek opportunities to innovate and improve The Ritz-Carlton experience.
6. I own and immediately resolve guest problems.
7. I create a work environment of teamwork and lateral service so that the needs of our guests and each other are met.
8. I have the opportunity to continuously learn and grow.

---

*The Ritz-Carlton Gold Standards are posted on their Web site at www.ritzcarlton.com/corporate/about_us/gold_standards.asp.

9. I am involved in the planning of the work that affects me.

10. I am proud of my professional appearance, language and behavior.

11. I protect the privacy and security of our guests, my fellow employees and the company's confidential information and assets.

12. I am responsible for uncompromising levels of cleanliness and creating a safe and accident-free environment.

[These service values, no doubt, build pride in The Ritz-Carlton, and they would serve any accounting or consulting firm well. The lesson? Ask yourself if your firm has values that are clearly stated and easy to understand. Just as these service values provide guidance to Ritz-Carlton employees about how to treat hotel guests and one another, your values should do the same.]

THE EMPLOYEE PROMISE

At The Ritz-Carlton, our Ladies and Gentlemen are the most important resource in our service commitment to our guests.

By applying the principles of trust, honesty, respect, integrity and commitment, we nurture and maximize talent to the benefit of each individual and the company.

The Ritz-Carlton fosters a work environment where diversity is valued, quality of life is enhanced, individual aspirations are fulfilled, and The Ritz-Carlton Mystique is strengthened.

[The Employee Promise represents the mutual contract between employees and the hotel.]

EXHIBIT 10–2   **Sample Form: Setting Performance Goals**

Employee Name: _____

Title: _____

Leader Name: _____

When it comes to performance goals for this year, what would *you* like to accomplish?

1. _____

2. _____

3. _____

Please rewrite your goals to ensure they are performance targets (that is, SMART goals: specific, measurable, achievable, relevant, and time-bound).

Direction Word	Performance Target	From	To	By

SAMPLE—SMART goals should be supported by SMART tasks.

	Direction Word	Performance Target	From	To	By
SMART Goal	Increase	Awareness of firm products/services	1 service	5 services	12/31/20XX
SMART Task #1	Improve	Attendance at firm's lunch 'n learn series	0 times per month	1 time per month	6/30/20XX
SMART Task #2					

	Direction Word	Performance Target	From	To	By
SMART Goal					
SMART Task #1					
SMART Task #2					

	Direction Word	Performance Target	From	To	By
SMART Goal					
SMART Task #1					
SMART Task #2					

	Direction Word	Performance Target	From	To	By
SMART Goal					
SMART Task #1					
SMART Task #2					

11

IS A PAY FOR PERFORMANCE SYSTEM RIGHT FOR YOU?

"There's nothing more unequal than the equal treatment of unequal people."

—Thomas Jefferson

When you think about the saying, "To steal second base, you must take your foot off first base" you may also think to yourself, "Yeah, and you can be thrown out if you do!" To determine whether a pay for performance compensation system (one in which pay decisions are based on defined performance levels rather than on entitlement, tenure, or other non-performance-related criteria) is right for you, you must be clear about what you hope to accomplish by having one. You must also be aware of the challenges and potential risks in moving to pay for performance.

PAY FOR PERFORMANCE CHALLENGES

Rich Rinehart, managing owner of Grant Owners and consultant to professional services firms, shared with us what an owner in a large regional firm in the Midwest told him, "I had the best year in my career last year. I sat down with our managing owner to go over this year's bonus and my base compensation for next year. I was elated with the result, the most money I've ever made. Then I asked to see the owner compensation schedule."

Rinehart believes whether you like it or not, compensation is absolute and relative in CPA firms, especially in the owner ranks. When firms move to performance-based compensation systems, they will necessarily compare one owner to another. As competitive creatures we all want to know how we did relative to our peer group. It has also been our experience there is an unwillingness and fear to look at one's own performance and performance relative to each other as owners. Human beings seem conflict-avoidant by nature, so the idea that we must talk about our compensation as an owner group or in individual meetings with managing owners strikes fear in the hearts of many CPAs. It's what often keeps many firms from changing their compensation structures from a traditional and increasingly archaic system. By working with owner groups on performance and compensation issues, we know we must help them look in the mirror or they may never change. For some firms, they *must* address pain (for example, poor performance or low compensation). For other firms, they *want* to address opportunities and *need* to develop strategies and goals to achieve them. Both scenarios often create the motivation to change their compensation systems.

We tell our clients to benchmark their financial performance against prior years, budgets, projections, competitors, and industry surveys. We tell them they need to compare where they are relative to their plans, their competition, and their industries. They are sometimes terrified to know the answers, and at the same time, cannot stand not knowing the answers. They want to know how they stack up relative to their fellow owners or relative to their CPA colleagues in other firms.

As firms move from traditional compensation systems to performance-based systems, they increasingly face the issue of owners comparing themselves to each other. There is a raging debate in firms today about whether to use open or closed compensation systems. Either way, comparison exists because owners (and employees) often know what others earn. Confidentiality about compensation is an illusion. When firms are looking at both objective, measurable factors as well as subjective, "soft" measures to determine owner compensation, developing reports that compare owner performance and compensation is key to driving and improving performance over time. The ultimate test of any compensation system is whether it will stand up to the scrutiny of the "absolute-relative" test by their owner groups.

Rinehart also provided us the following quote from one of his clients, the managing owner of a "top 100" firm:

> As long as I'm managing owner in this firm we will have an open owner compensation system. Owner bonus time is the one time during the year when I can sit down with each of my owners and explain to them how they are doing and what they need to do to improve. Our performance-based compensation system is the best tool I have to present the facts about performance in both absolute and relative terms.

This managing owner is obviously willing to have the difficult conversations that go along with owner compensation. Imagine football, basketball, or baseball games in which the score is not kept. How would it be to watch the games? What if there was no winner or loser, and at the end of the season, there was no Super Bowl, NBA Final, or World Series? In top performing firms, owners want to know where they stand and what they need to do to improve. Why not take the conversation about performance and compensation as an opportunity to do better next year? Help them understand how their performance influences their compensation.

In previous chapters, we discussed goal setting and aligning with firm vision, strategies, and goals. When we test our new compensation systems by exposing the "truth" about performance, both individually and as an owner group, we will necessarily come to the realization that no one person can carry the firm or be responsible for its success. As in sports, firm performance requires the efforts of a highly functional team. Relative compensation and well-designed compensation systems, like the performance they measure, tell you how you are doing. The reaction to how a group of owners performed in any given year should be cause to ask the question, How can we help each other do better next year? The notion that "rising tides float all boats" is worth pondering. If we see how others are performing and can help them perform better, we all make more money. In the end, by sharing absolute, as well as relative, compensation information, the understanding we gain about ourselves, our firms, and the future is worth the risk of offending someone or hurting their feelings. We cannot improve what we do not measure, and if we do not share it, debate it, and find out the truth about it we will never achieve the results we are looking for. Top firms know this is true and their results prove it.

PERFORMANCE-BASED COMPENSATION IS NOT A SILVER BULLET

Before we talk about performance targets, we must acknowledge the fact that there are as many consultants and practitioners who decry pay for performance systems as there are who support them. Even David Maister, a well-respected consultant to the accounting profession, said as recently as April 2006, "The disadvantage of pay for performance compensation systems is that they provide a wonderful excuse not to manage . . . By not paying for performance, you end up with higher performance by tackling performance issues."

Harvard Business School professor Michael Beer, has said, "Scholars have argued that the real problem is that incentives work too well. Specifically, they motivate employees to focus excessively on doing what they need to do to gain rewards, sometimes at the expense of doing other things that would help the organization."[1] Alfie Kohn, author of *Punished by Rewards: The Trouble With Gold Stars, Incentive Plans, A's, Praise, and Other Bribes*, says rewards may actually damage quality and productivity, and cause employees to lose interest in their jobs. Why? According to Kohn:

- Rewards control behavior through seduction. They are a way for people in power to manipulate those with less power.
- Rewards ruin relationships. They emphasize the difference in power between the person handing out the reward and the person receiving it.
- Rewards create competitiveness among employees, undermining collaboration and teamwork.
- Rewards reduce risk taking, creativity, and innovation. People will be less likely to pursue hunches, fearing such out-of-the-box thinking may jeopardize their chances for a reward.
- Rewards ignore reasons. A commission system, for example, may lead a manager to blame the sales staff when they do not meet quotas, when the real problem may be packaging or pricing.

---

[1]Michael Beer and Mark D. Cannon, *Promise and Peril in Implementing Pay for Performance: A Report on Thirteen Natural Experiments*, white paper, Vanderbilt University, 2007.

"Managers typically use a rewards system because it's easy," adds Kohn. "It doesn't take effort, skill or courage to dangle a doggie biscuit in front of an employee and say, 'Jump through this hoop and this will be yours.'"[2]

While we agree that all of the above comments by these authorities may be correct, we also agree with Jim Collins' findings in *Good to Great: Why Some Companies Make the Leap . . . and Others Don't* that a good compensation system helps recruit and retain great performers. A properly structured pay for performance system, therefore, may be the best thing out there. The goal of a pay for performance system is not to have the perfect system, but to better align compensation with performance and with the firm's strategic initiatives.

GETTING STARTED—DIAGNOSE BEFORE YOU DESIGN

There is, of course, no one right system for every firm. To develop the best system for your firm, utilize the framework of the Organizational Effectiveness Cycle (OEC), which we discussed in Chapter 3 to perform a diagnostic. Then consider (and answer!) the following questions:

- What specific *results* are you trying to get?
- What specific results do you want employees to get? (Refer to cascading goals.)
- What *behaviors* are needed from employees to get those results?
- What behaviors are you currently observing in your employees?
- What causes employees to refrain from engaging in the needed behaviors? (These causes are often called roadblocks.)
- What are you *doing as a firm* to motivate needed behaviors and remove roadblocks?
- *Why* are you doing each of the things you are doing?

The answers to these questions should serve as the necessary building blocks for constructing an effective compensation system—one that drives the results you identified by answering the first question. As you design your compensation system, you want to keep in mind the goals and attributes of an effective compensation system.

GOALS AND ATTRIBUTES OF AN EFFECTIVE COMPENSATION SYSTEM

Without a doubt, all firms are interested in significantly enhancing their ability to serve clients and other key stakeholders. The overarching goal of a compensation system is to encourage and motivate a full range of behaviors needed to do so. And to do so profitably, firms want work to flow where it will be done best, most quickly, and at the lowest cost (which achieves the most value for clients). Another common goal of a compensation system is to enable an organization to attract and retain qualified, competent workers. It should encourage capable senior associates and managers with an interest in firm ownership to *want* to become owners, to allow those who are capable and do not have an interest in ownership to be rewarded appropriately, and to encourage productive team members

---

[2]Alfie Kohn, *Punished by Rewards: The Trouble with Gold Stars, Incentive Plans, A's, Praise, and Other Bribes* (New York: Houghton Mifflin Company, 1999).

to stay with the firm until retirement. One of the ways it does this is by recognizing all types of contributions to the firm's success.

Finally, many firms want their compensation systems to be perceived as fair and equitable by those who are subject to it. For a plan to be successful, regardless of its implementation, employees must:

- Desire more pay
- Believe they will receive more pay if they improve their performance
- Trust the firm to administer the plan fairly

BUILDING A PAY FOR PERFORMANCE PLAN

By now you know there is no such thing as an off-the-shelf compensation plan. Here is a list of items to consider when building your plan:

- Who will participate in the plan (all employees or just owners)?
- How will the payouts be determined?
- How often will you make payouts?
- Will there be thresholds in order to get paid the bonus?
- Who will be responsible for administering the plan?
- What will your measures be?
- What will your targets be?
- How will you pay for the plan?
- Will the plan have any hold-back provisions?

An effective performance-based compensation plan rewards three areas that drive performance and results. Each of these reward areas is discussed in the following sections.

Rewards Both Character and Competence

Stephen R. Covey, in his highly acclaimed book, *The 7 Habits of Highly Effective People*, shares that personal trustworthiness is a combination of both character and competence. He quotes Gandhi as saying, "One man cannot do right in one department of life whilst he is occupied in doing wrong in any other department. Life is one indivisible whole."[3] When it comes to character, James F. Bracher, self-professed architect for the renewal of integrity-centered leadership, says, "Integrity-centered leadership is the only reliable foundation for long-term success!" Compensation should be tied to employees' demonstration of traits such as accountability, courtesy, determination, integrity, kindness, patience, respect, tolerance, and so on. It should also reward whether employees exhibit congruence between what they say and what they do, as well as what they say about what they did.

In addition to character, however, we must also consider competence. In his book, *Customers for Life*, Carl Sewell asserts that being nice to people is just 20 percent of providing good customer service. He also says, "All the smiles in the world aren't going to help you if your product or service

---

[3]Stephen R. Covey, *The 7 Habits of Highly Effective People* (New York: Fireside Press, 1989).

is not what the customer wants." Sewell further asserts that companies must design systems that allow you to do the job right the first time.[4] Most firm leaders would believe he is talking about work processes related to service delivery.

We believe training and development, performance management, and compensation systems are also necessary to facilitate an environment of empowerment in which employees *can* do it right the first time. Alexander L. Gabbin agrees. In his article, "The Crisis in Accounting Education: the CPA's Role in Attracting the Best and the Brightest to the Profession," he says, "Unlike the academic community, CPA firms were quick to realize that new business realities demanded a broader set of competencies."[5]

When we work with accounting firms, we find that firm leaders know what to do with employees who are either high in both character and competence or low in both character and competence—reward or terminate them respectively. The tough decisions arise when someone is high in character but low in competence, or low in character but high in competence. Firms are often tempted to retain those with high character and low competence because these employees are nice, and they hope their work product will get better over time. They are also tempted to retain those with low character and high competence because they produce high quality work in a timely fashion, even though they wreak havoc by making others miserable, or worse, place the firm at risk.

Based on effective evaluation, owners and employees can be placed in one of four quadrants, as illustrated in Exhibit 11–1, "The Character and Competence Matrix." Again, we hope everyone falls into quadrant 2. If not, however, it is easiest to help individuals move from quadrant 1 to quadrant 2. In the case of employees who reside in quadrant 1, we suggest a formal, individual development plan tied to compensation which gives employees a chance to improve competence over a relatively short (6 to 12 months) period of time.

In the case of employees who reside in quadrants 3 and 4 (low in character in both cases), it can be difficult to move them to either quadrant 1 or 2 respectively, regardless of the efforts to do so, including a formal, individual development plan tied to compensation that gives them a chance to improve in character. We argue it is key to ensure, during the hiring process, that potential employees are screened based on character attributes so there is less need to deal with a lack of character after employment. When it becomes necessary to do so, however, we suggest a plan for immediate and gracious departure if improvements in character (alignment with the firm's core values) are not forthcoming.

Rewards Both Leading and Lagging Measures of Success

When it comes to effective performance, it is important to understand the cause and effect between the varying behaviors and activities that help individuals achieve their desired results. To get a better handle on cause

---

[4]Carl Sewell, *Customers for Life* (New York: Currency by Doubleday, 1990).
[5]Alexander L. Gabbin, "The Crisis in Accounting Education: the CPA's Role in Attracting the Best and the Brightest to the Profession," *Journal of Accountancy*, April 2002.

and effect, we suggest a combination of both leading and lagging measures or indicators of success. Traditional individual accounting measures (for example, realization, utilization, new revenue, and so on) are lagging indicators of performance, and they report historic events. They represent the outcomes of actions that were taken in the past. In contrast, nonfinancial measures can be leading indicators of performance. Leading indicators usually measure processes and activities—those things that lead to (or drive) the lagging indicators. They often predict whether lagging measures will be achieved. For example, a decline in marketing-related activities is expected to lead to lower numbers of referrals from referral sources, and eventually a decline in new revenue. By the same token, an increase in strategic reviews of key clients is expected to drive more and deeper conversations with these clients about ways we can help them, and eventually an increase in cross-sold services.

Effective performance management is not just about collecting the right data. It is also about using data effectively to *drive* performance. Combining leading and lagging indicators provides executives with the tools they need to achieve this.

Rewards Both Independent and Interdependent Behaviors and Outcomes

Stephen R. Covey points out in *The 7 Habits of Highly Effective People*, "As we continue to grow and mature, we become increasingly aware that all of nature is *interdependent*, that there is an ecological system that governs nature, including society." *Independence* is the paradigm of *I*—*I* can do it; *I* am responsible; these are *my* goals. *Interdependence* is the paradigm of *we*—*we* can do it; *we* are responsible; these are *our* goals. When firms reward independence, they reward people for being self-reliant, developing their personal knowledge and skills, and hitting agreed-upon personal goals and objectives. When they reward interdependence, they reward people for being team players; developing others' personal knowledge and skills; and hitting agreed-upon team, departmental, or firm goals and objectives.

Covey goes on to say, "Interdependence is a choice only independent people can make. Dependent people cannot choose to become interdependent. This is a primary reason for rewarding independent behaviors. If we reward people for making good choices about their day-to-day behaviors, carrying out personal development plans, and accomplishing things that matter most, they develop a sense of personal value and contribution. This helps to increase their maturity even further and facilitates their choices about teaming with others to accomplish interdependent goals/objectives." The key is for the firm to be clear and specific about those interdependent goals and objectives.

When firms reward both, which is a more advanced concept, people begin to realize they can accomplish more by working together. When firms create an environment in which teamwork is encouraged and rewarded, a culture of true empowerment can be created.

STRUCTURING A PAY FOR PERFORMANCE COMPENSATION SYSTEM

Now that we have discussed *what* a performance-based compensation should reward, we will discuss *how* to do it. How do you *measure* character, competence, and successful goal accomplishment so you can reward owners and staff?

To measure the subjective "character" component, we suggest clarifying the firm's *core values* and defining what it looks like when employees are living them. This helps to take some of the subjectivity out of the measurement. To measure the also-subjective "competence" component, we also recommend clarifying and outlining the *competencies* one needs to perform his or her role in the firm. When measuring them, you will not evaluate whether individuals are *using* these competencies to help them accomplish independent or interdependent goals and objectives—only whether they *have* the competencies. By measuring "adherence to the firm's core values" and "development of competencies" you are measuring two wildly important leading indicators of success.

To measure "performance" objectively, we suggest you create *performance targets* that identify measurable behaviors (for example, engage in two client conversations in which you ask how your firm can improve its service to the client) as well as numeric, measurable goals and objectives (for example, production statistics)—both independent and interdependent. The following table provides an overview of the steps you can take to determine the structure for a performance-based compensation system.

Core Values	*Competencies*	*Performance Targets*
1. Determine the core values (examples may include integrity, continuous improvement, service excellence, teamwork, and so on).	1. Determine the competency categories (examples may include technical competencies, conceptual competencies, leadership and people development competencies, practice development competencies, client management competencies, practice management competencies, and so on).	1. Determine the performance target categories (these often mirror the competency categories described at left).
2. Define (in 12 to 20 words) what each core value means.		2. Define the objective performance target measures (both leading and lagging as well as both independent and interdependent) at the beginning of the evaluation year.
3. Describe what it looks like from a behavioral standpoint, if, in fact, people are living the values.		
4. Determine the weight (relative importance) of core values when determining its effect on compensation.	2. Define and describe the behavioral competencies within each of the competency categories.	
5. Evaluate, via a 360-degree review, how people are living the core values.		

Core Values	Competencies	Performance Targets
	3. Provide the appropriate resources and training so people can develop the needed competencies for their roles. 4. Determine the weight (relative importance) of each competency when determining its effect on compensation. 5. Evaluate at least annually whether people have the needed competencies for their roles.	3. Provide at least quarterly updates on how people are doing relative to their performance targets. 4. Evaluate annually whether people have accomplished their performance targets.

Each of these is discussed more completely in the sections that follow.

Why Measure Adherence to Core Values?

As firms face the challenges of an increasingly diverse workforce and constant change, it becomes more important for them to spell out their core values. This tells employees how they can expect to be treated, but it also tells them how the firm expects them to treat others. It tells them what they can count on, what the firm remains committed to over the long run. Well-defined and described core values let everyone know the price of admission. If you don't evaluate people on how they live the firm's core values, it can be easy for them to lose direction. By evaluating people against core value standards, you create awareness. Once individuals have awareness about how they are perceived by others to be living the core values, they can make choices about behavioral changes. When most, if not all, individuals in the firm engage in behaviors that adhere to the firm's core values, the desired culture is created.

Why Measure Development of Competencies?

In their book, *Competing for the Future*, authors Gary Hamel and C.K. Prahalad distinguished between an organization's core competencies and an individual's workplace competencies. They said an organization's core competencies "transcend any particular product or service, and indeed may transcend any single business unit within the organization."[6] In other words, some projects or services are so large (for example, an audit or specific consulting engagement) no individual can possess all the knowledge

---

[6]Gary Hamel and C.K. Prahalad, *Competing for the Future* (Boston: Harvard Business School, 1994), p. 201.

and skills needed to fulfill the project or service. Individual workplace competencies focus on employees and vary based on role in the firm (that is, they are specific to the position). For more than a century, accountants have been posting and balancing ledgers—requiring very specific and unique knowledge and skills (that is, competencies), most of which were learned on the job. In light of Frederick Taylor's "scientific management," Henry Ford's assembly line, and highly segmented work in the armed forces as well as command-and-control hierarchies found in the workforce, competencies were not emphasized.

In the early 1960s, David C. McClelland, a former Harvard psychologist and founder of McBer, asserted that I.Q. and personality tests then in common use were poor predictors of competency. He believed companies should hire based on competencies rather than test scores. Thus, companies slowly began to measure competence.

To measure competence, you must first define it. Firms are more equipped to drive business results when they define competencies by position and *then* (1) measure whether employees within the positions maintain those competencies and (2) develop those who lack the competencies. A competency table is simply an organizational structure that outlines, for each position in the firm, a set of competency categories (for example, communicates effectively, thinks strategically, coaches and develops others, and so on) as well as the specific knowledge and skills that are necessary within each competency category. Exhibit 11–2, "Sample Excerpt of a Competency Table," is a small excerpt from a competency table for a midsize firm. It illustrates that the ability to give presentations is an important competency within the "communicates effectively" competency category. Other specific competencies within the "communicates effectively" category might include the ability to write effective management reports, draft effective e-mail messages, or run an effective meeting. Exhibit 11–2 further illustrates that it is important for managers to be able to exhibit the specific behavior of preparing and assisting in the delivery of in-house and client presentations as well as the specific behavior of presenting proposals, budgets, and suggestions to principals and officers with regard to acceptance of prospective clients.

We suggest the use of competency tables for a variety of reasons, including the following:

- To help everyone understand position requirements
- To determine who should be interviewed for open positions
- To determine training needs based on lacking competencies
- To clarify why desired business results are not being met
- To understand what is necessary to move to the next level (that is, get promoted)
- To make more rational personnel decisions
- To increase overall competence in the workforce
- To create a healthier, more competitive firm
- To help stars stand out and prevent unqualified team members from hiding

Throughout this book we assert that employees who are not involved in the process of designing systems that will affect them generally lack commitment to the processes. We therefore strongly recommend you get employees involved in defining competencies. Why? Who is more knowledgeable about client needs and in the best position to satisfy those needs?

Both the AICPA and the Canadian Institute of Chartered Accountants (CICA) have developed skeleton competency tables. Exhibit 11–3, "AICPA Competencies," and Exhibit 11–4, "Canadian Institute of Chartered Accountants Competencies," may help you in developing your own competency tables.

Why Performance Targets?

According to Barry LaBov, CEO of LaBov & Beyond, a marketing communications firm, "People are people, and they want to be recognized. The programs that fail revolve around rewarding performance that doesn't support company goals. Improving sales performance, for example, is not enough. Today you need programs that support such issues as profitability, loyalty and customer satisfaction. And you have to do it without alienating other people within the organization." This supports our notion that the measurable objectives (that is, performance targets) must balance character and competence, leading and lagging measures, and independent and interdependent goals and objectives.

We actually agree with Alfie Kohn. "Rewards are a matter of doing things *to* employees. The alternative is working *with* employees, and that requires a better understanding of motivation and a transformation in how one looks at management." This is why we often refer to mutually agreed-upon performance targets as a win-win agreement. In addition to the balancing act described in the previous paragraph, performance targets are created mutually so all stakeholders get something as close as possible to a perfect "win" for them.

PROVIDING FEEDBACK IN A PAY FOR PERFORMANCE COMPENSATION SYSTEM

As we observed in Chapter 10, in any performance management system individuals should receive sufficient feedback to know where their performance is strong and where they require improvement. Agreeing on the measures at the beginning of the year and then waiting a year later to see whether they were accomplished is woefully insufficient. Feedback should be provided at least quarterly.

However, it is not enough to let employees know regularly where they stand. They must believe in the metrics that are used as well as the tools that measure the metrics. As the old saying goes, "Garbage in; garbage out." When employees do not trust the measurement tools, the data or information that goes into the tools, or the individuals who input the data, their cynicism increases. When cynicism increases, employees often throw up their hands in disgust and settle into a performance level that seems acceptable to them.

TRANSLATING PERFORMANCE INTO COMPENSATION

We have observed throughout this book that a firm must identify measures that guide everyday employee decision-making. Employees need to know what specific actions they can take to ensure that expectations are met or exceeded. Unfortunately, however, the link between superior performance and compensation remains weak. In addition to establishing the *criteria* on which performance will be rewarded, you must determine the *mechanism* for monetary rewards. The following are three common possibilities, each of which rewards both character and competence, both leading and lagging measures, and both independent and interdependent goals and objectives:

- *Annual salary increase* based on a cost-of-living or market increase plus living the firm's core values, developing competency within themselves, and achieving a variety of objective measures.
- *Annual salary increase* (based on cost-of-living and/or market increase) *plus annual bonus* based on a combination of criteria, including living the firm's core values, developing competency within themselves, and achieving a variety of objective measures.
- *Annual salary increase* (based on cost-of-living and/or market increase) *plus multiple bonuses* based on living the firm's core values, developing competency within themselves, and achieving a variety of objective measures.

EFFECTS OF A PAY FOR PERFORMANCE COMPENSATION SYSTEM

The net effect of a good pay for performance compensation system should be the same for employees as it is for owners. You should expect the following benefits from a well-designed system:

- Compensation increases are based on overall contribution to the success of the firm rather than one or two measures of success.
- The system creates a results-driven, performance culture, rather than a culture of entitlement.
- Employees and owners know with clarity their:
  —Job descriptions at each level
  —Career progression opportunities within the firm
  —Compensation upside
  —Personal goals which they help to create
  —Performance reviews

All of this leads to greater personal accountability, which in turn should lead to higher levels of productivity, efficiencies, and profitability.

FINAL THOUGHTS

When you try something new, you can almost be sure it will not be perfect the first time. The same is true for compensation programs. To come as close as possible to perfection, however, here are things you need to consider:

- What factors will be part of your new plan? Determine what factors you will measure and how you will measure them. The factors on which people will be measured should motivate them to behave in a manner that furthers the firm's strategic initiatives.
- What weight will you assign for each factor? Depending on your strategic initiatives, the factors on which you measure should have different weights, and the weights can and should change from year to year based on changes in your strategic initiatives.
- What tool(s) will you use to measure each factor? You can use 360-degree surveys, productivity reports from the time and billing system, marketing reports, satisfaction surveys, and a wide variety of other tools to measure the factors.
- Does the compensation system recognize all types of contribution to the firm's success? Firms need strong finders, minders, and grinders as well as leaders, mentors, coaches, and so on to be successful. Firms are a composite of the knowledge, skills, and personal attributes of their owners and employees. Fortunately, people are not clones of one another, and your compensation system needs to recognize the various contributions that drive the firm's overall success. While it is true that not everyone is created equal, it is also true that your firm would not be where it is today without everyone contributing, in some fashion, to its success.
- Is it perceived to be fair? A system that is not perceived to be fair or fairly applied is doomed to cause problems. We suggest, therefore, that you seek feedback at least annually to determine existing beliefs about the compensation system's fairness.
- Is it flexible to meet changing needs of the firm? Firms definitely change and you want to ensure the program is flexible enough to change along with the firm. We are not suggesting frequent changes in the compensation system, however. We suggest changes only to the degree they are absolutely necessary.
- Does it have significant differentials in compensation from owner to owner (or team member to team member)? Small variances in total compensation (that is, salary + bonus) between people in the same role (especially senior roles) are not healthy. As we said, owners and employees are not clones, nor do they contribute equally. The longer your system is in place, the greater the gap in compensation between the highest performer and the lowest performer in each level at the firm.

EXHIBIT 11–1   **The Character and Competence Matrix**

High Character Low Competence ①	② High Character High Competence
Low Character Low Competence ③	④ Low Character High Competence

EXHIBIT 11–2   **Sample Excerpt of a Competency Table**

Communicates Effectively—Presentations

Write-Up	Junior	Semi-Senior	Senior	Manager	Senior Manager	Principal	Owner
Can assist with internal presentations when required.	Can assist with internal presentations when required.	Can prepare and assist in the delivery of in-house presentations.	Can prepare and assist in the delivery of in-house and client presentations.	Can prepare and deliver in-house and client presentations. Can present proposals, budgets and suggestions to principals and officers with regard to acceptance of prospective clients.	Can present in-house and client presentations and coach others on how to present information. Can present proposals to current or prospective clients.	Can present in-house and client presentations and coach others on how to present information. Can present proposals to current or prospective clients.	Can present in-house and client presentations and coach others on how to present information. Can present proposals to current or prospective clients.

EXHIBIT 11–3   **AICPA Competencies**

- Interpersonal skills and awareness
- Networking and dynamics
- Motivation and leadership
- Organizational
- Communication
- Quantitative
- Critical thinking

- Abstract and adapt
- Learning and training
- Information technology
- Global and external awareness
- Ethical/legal environment of management
- Technical

EXHIBIT 11–4   Canadian Institute of Chartered Accountants Competencies

- The pervasive qualities and skills, which include:

  — Ethical behavior and professionalism

  — Personal attributes such as accountability; adaptability to change; and the ability to self-manage, take initiative, and add value

  — Professional skills such as communication, problem solving, and management skills

- The specific competencies (grouped into six categories):

  — Organizational effectiveness, control, and risk management

  — Finance

  — Taxation

  — Assurance

  — Performance measurement

  — Information and information technology

12

PAY FOR PERFORMANCE: ALIGN COMPENSATION TO FIRM INITIATIVES

"While many compensation systems are constructed to be fair, few are ever constructed to be strategic."

—August Aquila

According to a white paper titled "Best Practices in Recruiting and Retaining Talented Staff," from the AICPA Private Companies Practice Section, the AICPA Alliance for CPA Firms, 75 percent of responding firms do not have a documented pay for performance plan that aligns compensation with firm strategic initiatives. The fact that 53 percent of the firms responding to our 2006 Compensation Survey do not tie owner compensation to achievement of their strategic plans was one of the most surprising findings. Almost 10 percent of the firms responding to our survey tie compensation to achievement of their strategic plans, and the rest (37.5 percent) responded by saying the owner compensation system is tied to achievement of the strategic plan to some extent.

As a result of Coral's work with Conner Ash P.C., we have evidence that firms can significantly increase net income per owner when owners and employees are aligned with the firm's strategic plan and have cascading performance goals. According to Howard Rosen, principal and president, "The results have been better than we ever expected. Our associates have really embraced the program, and everyone's income is up far more than would have otherwise been possible. Nonowner bonuses have averaged more than 17 percent of compensation, and owner income has risen 75 percent in two years. Paying for performance, or *rewarding for results* as we call it at Conner Ash, has been a great tool for recruiting as well as retention."

While there are different ways to tie the compensation system to achieving the strategic plan, developing cascading goals and using a pay for performance system are usually best because you reward owners and employees for achieving the firm's business objectives in such a plan. Because a pay for performance system rewards the firm's above-average performers more than average and below-average performers, it is also an effective way to motivate top performers to stay with the firm. In today's tight job market, one high performer may be worth two or more mediocre or average performers.

ONLY PERFORMANCE IS REALITY

Harold Geneen, former CEO of ITT, said, "In business, words are words, explanations are explanations, promises are promises, but only performance is reality." If we agree with Harold Geneen, then it seems we need to reward for strategy implementation and performance.

Firms have been struggling for years to get better performance from their owners and employees. This is often because they cannot see the alignment amongst mission, vision, strategy, and systems, and they do not know completely what they need to do on a day-to-day basis to help achieve that alignment. As discussed in Chapter 3, the Organizational Effectiveness Cycle is one tool you can use to better align the firm, by helping everyone see alignment and effect it. We often remind our clients that "all firms are perfectly aligned to get the results they get." The first step to getting alignment with mission and vision is to communicate the mission, vision, and values and what successful performance looks like.

Finally, firm performance is driven by execution or implementation of its strategic initiatives. Execution is a discipline that firm leaders must learn. While most firms are getting better at creating strategic plans, many still suffer from poor implementation of the plan.

ALIGN COMPENSATION TO STRATEGIC GOALS

If you want to drive results (performance) in your firm, align owner and employee compensation to the firm's strategic initiatives. Before you even get started down that road, however, be sure you and your fellow owners have answered the following questions:

- Do we have a shared vision for the firm?
- Can everyone in the firm clearly state it in 25 words or fewer?
- Do we have one firm culture or many cultures in the firm?
- Have we identified the three or four most important goals the firm needs to accomplish this year?
- How many people in the firm know what the three or four most important goals are?
- Have we identified what success looks like in each one of these goals?
- Do we know how motivated the owners and staff are to achieve these goals?
- Do we know how committed the owners and staff are to achieving these goals?

No discussion about pay for performance is complete without examples of firms that experienced paradigm shifts and then created and implemented such systems as a result. You will note that each system varies, but all have the ultimate goal of aligning performance with strategic initiatives.

REAL-LIFE EXAMPLE ONE—A FIRM IN TRANSITION

In early 2003, Conner Ash P.C. was continuing to undergo transition—the impending retirement of its managing principal, the hiring of a very capable tax principal, and the need for a shared vision in terms of niche development and people development. When Coral began working with the firm, its short-term goals were to:

1. Clarify mission and vision.
2. Create a strategic plan to support the mission and vision that included:
   a. A subplan for transition from soon-to-be-retired owners to new owners
   b. A marketing and advertising strategy
   c. An analysis of current operations and how the firm compared to similar firms
   d. A clear understanding of what distinguished the firm from the pack
3. Refine existing systems and processes to support the strategic plan.

The first two goals were completed in 2003. For four years, the firm has been committed to its mission "to provide high-quality accounting and business advisory services that help our clients achieve what matters most to them and to do so in a manner that exceeds their expectations." In accomplishing its mission, Conner Ash team members have made a commitment to, and are evaluated on, living the firm's core values:

- Our family members are owners in our success.
- We enjoy ourselves.
- We are profitable.
- We have integrity.
- We value continuous learning.
- We are timely.
- We communicate consistently.

The third goal (systems and processes refinement) was completed throughout 2003 and 2004, the most significant refinement being the design, development, and implementation of a compensation system for both owners and employees that rewards for results. As previously noted, the firm's associates embraced the program, and everyone's income has increased far more than would have otherwise been possible.

While each owner and staff member has individually developed win-win agreements, one owner's agreement was based on the following criteria:

- Personal Stewardship
  —*Client Development*
    - Extras (cross-sold) *$$*
    - New *$$* developed or co-developed
  —*Client Management*
    - Client meetings attended
    - SpotLight™ letters delivered and discussed
  —*Business Management*
    - Personal charge hours
    - Days of lock-up (A/R and WIP)
    - Client work completed by agreed-upon date
    - Keep tax department within budget

- Firm-wide Stewardship
  —*Coordinate planning for upcoming tax season*
  - Software—ensure all items ready (rollover, e-file, practice aide)
  - Training—develop and implement
  - Coordinate needs of professional staff and support
  —*Begin development of tax department identity*
  —*Get 401(k) plan document in place; ensure all participants receive info*
  —*Niche marketing (play visible role in transportation and pension plan marketing programs)*
  —*Be a strong referral source* (measured by number of referrals)
  —*Ensure mentoring program is in place*

REAL-LIFE EXAMPLE TWO—ONE MANAGING OWNER'S WAKE-UP CALL

According to Michael Epstein, the managing partner of Toronto-based accounting firm Fuller Landau, LLP, his wake-up call came in the year 2000. Two things happened. First, he realized nowhere near enough time was spent on people matters, despite it being the number one challenge to his firm. Second, Michael became familiar with the *service profit chain*, which is the notion that firm profitability and growth is tied directly to client satisfaction and loyalty as well as employee loyalty, satisfaction, and productivity. There is a direct relationship between happy people and clients *and* profits.

The authors of *The Service Profit Chain*[1] discovered that "the strongest relationships are those between (1) profit and customer loyalty; (2) employee loyalty and customer loyalty; and (3) employee satisfaction and customer satisfaction. Moreover, these relationships are mutually reinforcing; that is, satisfied customers contribute to employee satisfaction and vice versa." The service profit chain is outlined in the following chart (see p. 155).

The authors believe that this is the foundation for a powerful strategic service vision; a model on which any leader or manager can build more focused operations and marketing capabilities. For example, the authors demonstrate how, in Banc One's operating divisions, a direct relationship between customer loyalty, which is measured by the *depth* of a relationship (the number of banking services a customer utilizes), and profitability led the bank to encourage existing customers to further extend the bank services they use. The authors of *The Service Profit Chain* describe how companies in any service industry can:

1. Measure service profit chain relationships across operating units.
2. Communicate the resulting self-appraisal.
3. Develop a balanced scorecard of performance.
4. Develop a recognitions and rewards system tied to established measures.

---

[1]James L. Heskett, W. Earl Sasser, Jr., and Leonard A. Schlesinger, *The Service Profit Chain*. New York: The Free Press, 1997.

5. Communicate results across the company.
6. Develop an internal best practice information exchange.
7. Improve overall service profit chain performance.

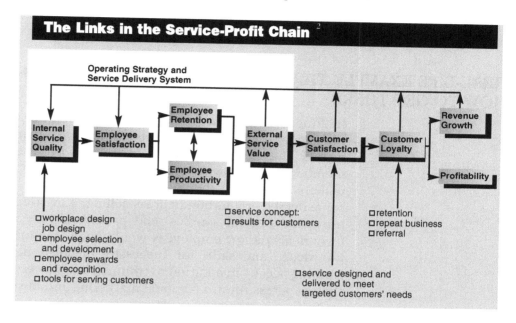

The Links in the Service-Profit Chain [2]

As a result of a detailed understanding of the service profit chain and acknowledgment of some of the people, development, and management mistakes he and the firm had made in the past (for example, not following up on an employee satisfaction survey or having an owner rather than a human resources professional handle people and people systems), Epstein modified his and his firm's journey toward making a difference. He knew it would be important to develop a firm-wide recognition and rewards system tied to established measures, that is, pay for performance. He also knew it would be critical for people to do what, in their minds, matters most to them, as long as it matters to the firm. Finally, he knew the firm needed help in designing, developing, and implementing the system. Coral is honored to have had the opportunity to work with Epstein and the firm's human resources director, Jennifer King, in creating a system that exactly meets the firm's needs.

According to Epstein, a number of paradigms are required to build such a system:

■ Leaders with a passion for people and an understanding of the importance that building relationships plays in such a system
■ Genuine interest in making people a priority
■ Deep understanding of who the firm's people are and what they expect from the firm (which is no different than taking time to understand what clients want)

---

[2]Reprinted by permission of *Harvard Business Review*. The Links in the Service-Profit Chain from "Putting the Service-Profit Chain to Work" by James L. Heskett, Thomas O. Jones, Gary W. Loveman, W. Earl Sasser, Jr., and Leonard A. Schlessinger, March/April, 1994. Copyright © 1994 by Harvard Business School Publishing Corporation; all rights reserved.

The system has been in place for two years, and minor refinements have been implemented. According to King, "The great thing about this system is our ability to tailor it to our firm's culture and to adjust it periodically to reward the activities that are important at the time, usually those that make the firm more profitable."

REAL-LIFE EXAMPLE THREE—NEEDED: FIRM GROWTH; CHALLENGE: HOW TO GET THERE

In June 1999, Meyners + Co., LLC, lost one of its rainmaker owners to retirement, highlighting the need to develop a marketing culture that supported the remaining, already-stretched owner group. Only a few members of the owner group considered themselves to be strong rainmakers. The firm, therefore, decided to get all employees involved, to some degree or another, in cross-selling to existing clients, developing and nurturing referral sources, and prospecting for new clients. The firm's owners also knew employees would need training to develop the needed knowledge and skills for successful business development. Hence, the training began! In addition to training, employees were also asked to track their progress toward personal marketing and business development goals and report periodically to an outside consultant who would, in turn, report to firm management. Nothing changed.

When the Growth Partnership, Inc., was asked in 2001 to assist Meyners + Co. with its marketing initiatives, we gathered a wide variety of data—both statistical and anecdotal—about the firm's growth, business goals, niches, services, and people development systems to support it all. In short, we found there was no way for the firm to handle the additional work we believed we could help them win. The firm had neither the time nor infrastructure needed to provide the level of client services that it so strongly believed in. It also needed clarity on its mission, vision, and core values, and it needed well-tuned people development, performance management, and compensation systems to drive its goals. The owners at Meyners + Co. agreed.

After the firm gained clarity on its mission and vision, we assisted the firm in defining:

- Core values (and how to evaluate whether employees are living them)
- Specific, measurable goals and objectives for each person that drive desired business results
- Competencies needed to achieve the specific goals and objectives

In short, we helped the firm design, develop, and implement its first pay for performance system, but not without some additional findings. After two years, based on user evaluations of the system, it became apparent that system administration (bonus calculations and paperwork) of an otherwise well-designed compensation system was not as simple as it needed to be. We share this learning with you as advice to keep the paperwork and bonus calculations manageable.

REAL-LIFE EXAMPLE FOUR—TIERED REWARD SYSTEM

In the June 2002 issue of the *Journal of Accountancy*, Michael Hayes, Senior Editor, discusses several firms, their pay for performance systems, and how they keep track and reward owner productivity.[3] One of the firms is Stambaugh Ness, P.C.

Stambaugh Ness, P.C., uses a tiered reward system that focuses on seven performance areas (business development, book production, billable hours, hours managed, realization, managing the firm, and process improvement). This system is outlined in Exhibit 12–1, "Sample Tiered Pay for Performance System."

As in any effective pay for performance system, owners compete with themselves and not with each other—the system promotes a win-win environment of mutual benefit rather than a win-lose or lose-lose environment in which scarcity exists. The maximum score any single principal can achieve is 400, and the firm monitors performance during the year using objective data. According to Hayes, the executive committee evaluates owners based on the data. The firm also asks for grades from clients as well as staff members.

The five factors at the bottom of the chart (account management; personal planning; recording time; situations, opportunities, and concerns; and firm support) are considered *hygiene issues*. Owners do not get rewarded for performing these activities, but penalties exist if they do not perform in these areas. Each of the five factors has a total weight of 20 points. Hence, an owner can lose up to 100 points (20 points × 5 areas).

At Stambaugh Ness, P.C., annual owner compensation comprises two components. The first—an equal base amount for all owners—is multiplied by the total number of owners. The firm compares that base-salary total with the firm's owner-compensation budget. The difference becomes the firm's incentive and bonus pools. Owners must achieve a minimum score of 250 to be included in the bonus pool. The firm's goal is to reduce the base salary each year.

There is only one drawback in this approach. It fails to reward owners for building future capacity in the firm. While the hygiene factors are important, they fail to address such needs as training, mentoring, coaching, systems development, and refinement.

REAL-LIFE EXAMPLE FIVE—COMPENSATION SYSTEM IN A MID-SIZED FIRM

A mid-size firm with five owners asked us for assistance in developing a pay for performance system for the owners. They wanted to develop a new compensation plan that could be implemented over the next several years. After gaining an understanding of their needs and what they were willing to embrace, we proposed the following plan.

We started with the previous year's total owner compensation and agreed upon a percentage of that amount as total base compensation for the current year. We called their base salaries Level 1 compensation. The

---

[3]Michael Hayes, "Pay for Performance," *Journal of Accountancy* (June 2002).

owners felt comfortable taking 77 percent of the previous year's total compensation as their Level 1 draws (salaries). They estimated the current year's net income and decided to allocate the difference between net income and Level 1 draws to a *performance pool*. This performance pool was Level 2 compensation.

Note: When firms take this approach, we usually recommend they allocate approximately 75 percent to base salaries and 25 percent to the performance pool (Level 2 compensation) during the first year of the new system. The goal is to continue to lower the base salary and increase bonus opportunities over time. Because most owners will not receive 100 percent of their bonus potential, a third level of pay was developed to reward owners who have an extraordinary year. Here is an example of how this would be calculated.

Let us assume that in the previous year, total owner compensation was $1.3 million. For the current year, the firm decides to distribute to the owners 77 percent ($1,003,000), which is allocated based on the previous year's draws. This leaves $497,000 for the performance pool or a potential of $99,400 in bonus for each of 5 owners. Each owner has an individual scorecard or win-win agreement with the firm. There is an example of this in Exhibit 12–2, "Sample Compensation in a Mid-Sized Firm."

The owner in the example received $82,502 of the potential bonus of $99,400. It is important to note that each owner in this system must reach a minimum level of performance in each area to receive the bonus amount for that area. The difference between the potential bonus amount and the amount the owner actually received is returned to the performance pool for distribution at Level 3 (extraordinary performance), which is discretionary and mutually-agreed upon by all owners.

The key here is that each owner had different tangible (objective) and intangible (subjective) goals to achieve.

REAL-LIFE EXAMPLE SIX—USING THE BALANCED SCORECARD

As we saw in Chapter 5, the Balanced Scorecard usually focuses on 4 key areas (financial, client, employee, and internal systems and business processes). Developing a compensation system based on accomplishment within each of these areas is not difficult. The real danger is having too many objectives and measures within each of the key areas.. For example, if you have 4 areas and 2 or 3 objectives in each one, you have created 8 to 12 key measures. Twelve is definitely on the high side, especially for the first year of implementing the Balanced Scorecard and new compensation system. We suggest you limit firm-wide goals to a total of 5 to 7 key measures that will drive the best results for the firm.

Let us look at the example included as Exhibit 12–3, "Firm Objectives." The firm has six objectives in four areas. Each objective is given a performance target. The target defines success. Finally, the firm decides what weight to allocate to each objective. Exhibit 12–3 shows the area, firm-wide objective, target, weight, and the actual performance of our hypothetical firm.

In this example, the firm has agreed to pay each person in the firm a bonus of up to 10 percent of his or her compensation, provided the firm achieves or exceeds the targets it sets for itself. In the exhibit, the firm achieved its objectives related to revenue growth, profitability increase, client satisfaction, and employee satisfaction. The firm failed to achieve its employee turnover and reduction in turn-around time objectives. As a result, the firm will pay each person in the firm 70 percent of his or her potential bonus. In this case, the firm is paying for firm performance, so even average and below-average performers benefit.

Even when firms develop scorecards for the firm, they often fail to develop scorecards for each owner and employee. We believe this is a mistake. Individual scorecards with objectives in each of the four areas—that tie to the firm's objectives—should be created. Examples of three scorecards are included in Exhibit 12–4, "Sample Firm-Wide Balanced Scorecard;" Exhibit 12–5, "Sample Owner Balanced Scorecard;" and Exhibit 12–6, "Sample Manager Balanced Scorecard."

FINAL THOUGHTS

As the examples demonstrate, there are countless ways to share the compensation pie. What works in one firm may not work in another. With this in mind, we end this chapter with the following keys to success when developing your pay for performance compensation system:

1. Diagnose before you prescribe. When you visit your doctor with symptoms, he or she must diagnose before prescribing medication or treatment. Be sure you know the underlying problems—not just the symptoms—of your current plan.
2. Understand that individual behavior drives firm-wide culture. Each firm will design its own compensation program, and it should motivate individuals to live the firms' values, develop their competencies, and hit their performance goals, thus creating the desired culture. Your compensation plan will not change the firm's culture, so make sure you start with developing the culture you want and then design the compensation plan to support that culture.
3. Involve everyone in the diagnosis and design; get their input. Involvement is absolutely essential for a successful program. We often say, "No involvement, no commitment." This does not mean, however, you must gain consensus. The ultimate decision rests with the firm's management team.
4. Be sure *everyone* understands the new plan and owners buy into it. You cannot spend too much time educating staff members and owners about their programs. They must understand how it will work, how it will be funded, and who will administer it.
5. Keep it simple. It is quite easy to make the compensation system more complicated than it needs to be.

EXHIBIT 12–1 **Sample Tiered Pay for Performance System[1]**

| | Principal A | | | Principal B | | | Principal C | | | Principal D | | | Principal E | | |
	Weight	Score	Total	Weight	Score	Total	Weight	Score	Total	Weight	Score	Total	Weight	Score	Total
Business development	0	0	0	10	8	80	0	0	0	0	0	0	0	0	0
Book production	10	5	50	10	7	70	10	6	60	10	10	100	10	4	40
Billable hours	10	7	70	5	9	45	3	8	24	4	6	24	10	3	30
Hours managed	10	7	70	5	8	40	7	7	49	6	8	48	5	5	25
Realization	10	10	100	10	7	70	10	6	60	10	6	60	10	4	40
Managing the firm	0	0	0	0	0	0	10	7	70	0	0	0	0	0	0
Process improvement	0	0	0	0	0	0	0	0	0	10	7	70	5	6	30
	40	29	290	40	39	305	40	34	263	40	37	302	40	22	165
Account Management	–4	0	0	–4	6	–24	–4	0	0	–4	0	0	–4	8	–32
Personal planning	–2	5	–10	–2	0	0	–2	0	0	–2	0	0	–2	5	–10
Recording time	–2	0	0	–2	3	–6	–2	0	0	–2	0	0	–2	0	0
Situations, opportunities, concerns	–2	7	–14	–2	3	6	–2	0	0	–2	0	0	–2	4	–8
Firm support	–10	8	–80	–10	0	0	–10	0	0	–10	0	0	–10	4	–40
	–20	20	–104	–20	12	–36	–20	0	0	–20	0	0	–20	21	–90
Totals			186			269			263			302			75

Account management includes monthly billing, timely and accurate submission of information and assistance with account collection. Time is recorded daily. Firm support includes promotion of film initiatives, use of proprietary software, checklists and processes, setting an example (dedication, positive attitude, attendance and professional behavior) and meeting schedules.

Scores		Bonus pool = ฿50,000			Incentive allocation pool = ฿150,000			
						Allocation	Base salary	Total
Principal D	302	36.21%	฿18,106		27.58%	฿41,370	฿80,000	฿121,370
Principal B	269	32.25%	16,127		24.57%	36,849	80,000	116,849
Principal C	263	31.53%	15,767		24.02%	36,027	80,000	116,027
Principal A	182				16.99%	25,479	80,000	105,479
Principal E	75				6.85%	10,274	80,000	90,274
Total points	1,095	100.00%	฿50,000		100.00%	฿150,000	฿400,000	฿550,000

[1]Reprinted with permission. Stambaugh Ness, P.C.

EXHIBIT 12–2   Sample Compensation in a Mid-Sized Firm

Level 2 Compensation—Performance Pool

Dollar amount available for performance factors $497,000

	Goal	Weight	Achieved	Payout	Min to get Payout
Objective Factors		55%			
Billable hours	1375	35%	1307	35%	95%
Book of Business/Clients Managed					
Sub-Category #1: Net Realization—Tax	92%	10%	88%	10%	95%
Sub-Category #2: Net Realization—Business					
Valuation and Litigation Support	85%	10%	75%	0%	95%
Cultural Factors		10%			
Living the Core Values	80%	10%	100%	10%	80%
Building Capacity Factors		0%			
					90%
Business Development Factors		25%			
Bus Val/Lit Support work	$175,000	25%	$175,000	25%	0%
Seniority Factor (weight no more than 10%)		10%			
1% for each yr as partner to a max of 10 yrs	10	10%	3	3%	1
	Possible	100%	Achieved	83%	$82,502.00

LEVEL 3 (OPTIONAL)—SPECIAL SUBJECTIVE BONUS ALLOCATION (Extraordinary Performance)
                                                                                    $ -

EXHIBIT 12–3   **Firm Objectives**

Area	Objective	Target	Weight	Actual Performance
Financial	Revenue growth	20%	20%	20%
Financial	Profitability increase	6% points	20%	6%
Client	Improve satisfaction	85%	10%	86%
Employee	Improve satisfaction	85%	20%	85%
Employee	Reduce turnover	5% or less	20%	6%
Business process	Reduce turn-around time	10% decrease	10%	8%
Firm total			100%	

EXHIBIT 12–4 Sample Firm-Wide Balanced Scorecard

Area	Objective	Target	Weight	Actual Performance
Financial	Increase revenue growth	20%	20%	
Financial	Increase net income	6% points	20%	
Client	Improve client satisfaction scores	85%	20%	
Employee growth and learning	Satisfaction	85%	25%	
Internal systems and business processes	Implement a uniform tax preparation process	12/31/XX	15%	
	Install CRM program	12/31/XX		
Firm total			100%	

Exhibit 12–5   **Sample Owner Balanced Scorecard**

Area	Objective	Target	Weight	Actual Performance
Financial	Increase new business development	20%	20%	
Financial	Increase managed book of business to $1.1 million	$1.1M	20%	
Client	Implement client development plans for top 20 clients	20 clients	20%	
Employee growth and learning	■ Serve on employee training and development committee. ■ Assist in developing manager and senior manager competency tables	12 meetings 2 tables	25%	
Internal systems and business processes	Chair the tax preparation processing committee	Finalized by 12/31/XX	15%	
Firm total			100%	

EXHIBIT 12–6   **Sample Manager Balanced Scorecard**

Area	Objective	Target	Weight	Actual Performance
Financial	Increase personal production to $185,000	20%	20%	
Financial	Acquire 5 new clients	5	20%	
Client	Improve client satisfaction scores	85%	20%	
Employee	Obtain CVA certificate Prepare business valuation course for seniors	12/31/XX 6/30/XX	25%	
Business process	Serve on CRM committee		15%	
Firm total			100%	

13

COMPENSATING THE MANAGING OWNER

> "In many firms, the managing partner title is utilized to describe a person who is really an administrative partner with no real power to 'manage' the firm (or other partners). In contrast, a true managing partner is the key person in achieving the firm's financial and other goals."
>
> —Stephen Weinstein, CPA

We are often asked, when developing compensation plans for firms, "What's a managing owner worth?" While we are unsure about the definitive answer to this question, there is a different question we *can* answer: "What should a managing owner be doing?" Only when a firm has a clear understanding of the managing owner role and the expectations of the incumbent is it possible to determine what the individual should be paid and how.

Determining compensation for the managing owner of a small firm is generally less difficult than determining it for a managing owner in a larger firm because the managing owner in a small firm usually maintains a book of business and is evaluated on similar criteria as other owners. In larger firms, however, where the managing owner may have little or no billable time, compensation becomes a more complex issue.

Some of the issues with which larger firms struggle include:

- What happens if the managing owner wants to step down early?
- If so, does the managing owner rebuild his or her client base?
- What type of security or safety net does the managing owner have?
- What happens if owners believe the managing owner is not meeting expectations?

WHAT IS A MANAGING OWNER WORTH?

You can ask 20 people this question and get as many answers. Before you can determine what to pay your managing owner, you need to clarify the role and outline expectations. Does your managing owner serve as the CEO of the firm or as a highly paid administrator? Over the years, we have asked several managing owners what they do. We share three responses.

Example One—Steve Mayer

Steve Mayer, CPA, is the managing owner of Burr Pilger & Mayer, a progressive firm in San Francisco. BPM was founded in 1986 by three 10-year managers from Coopers & Lybrand. Since that time it has grown to 130 employees, approximately $20 million in revenue, three offices, and 16 owners. As a full-service firm, its offerings include HR consulting, IT consulting, and write-up services. It also maintains an SEC practice (20 public companies) and a wealth management practice with insurance and investment advisory services.

This is what Steve had to say:

I have a very strong opinion about the role of the managing owner. Of course, a lot depends on the size of the firm, the abilities of the current owners, and whether the firm is in its first generation or has already made a transition from its founders. I have functioned as the managing owner since the beginning of Burr Pilger & Mayer (BPM). Here are some of my key points on the subject of the role of the managing owner.

1. The managing owner is the key leader of the firm. He or she sets the tone of the personality of the firm, helps to build the vision, implements the strategic plan, and leads by example.
2. The managing owner must continue to motivate and challenge the older owners, while teaching and training the younger owners on their future roles in the firm.
3. The managing owner must be perceived by the staff as the right person to lead the firm. The staff must have confidence in the managing owner's leadership ability or they won't buy into the vision.
4. The managing owner must have the courage to spend dollars wisely and build the correct infrastructure to support the firm's activities. Whether marketing, internal accounting, IT, human resources, and/or office services, the support staff is critical to the success of the firm. Many managing owners consider this overhead. We consider these costs the glue that keeps BPM together.
5. The managing owner needs to be an excellent client service owner—creative and a strong advocate for the client. Others in the firm must be impressed with the technical ability of the managing owner in serving clients, otherwise he or she is just another person with a "do as I say and not as I do" approach to life.
6. The managing owner must be a hard worker but demonstrate balance in life. A workaholic serves no purpose, nor does someone who is golfing every day. The balance between working at the office, family life, vacation, and community service is vital to the balance of life.
7. I believe that until the firm is over 200 people, the managing owner needs a decent-sized book of business. It is difficult to maintain a large book of business and perform the other roles of managing owner, but $750K to $1.5M is doable depending on the size of the clients. It is also important to set the example on collections, realization and cross-selling to clients.
8. The managing owner must set the tone for the firm's involvement in the community. Every company should have as a building block of its existence a commitment to the community. I believe a CPA firm is uniquely

situated to have all its owners and most of its staff involved in the community to get the firm's name out there.

9. The managing owner needs to make sure the firm, through its annual events or just its day-to-day operations, is a fun place to work. Parties, firm activities, special days off, and office decorations—all add to the firm's personality. To attract and retain good people, the firm needs to be a fun place to work.

10. The managing owner needs to have a system of accountability for all employees (including owners) that measures and evaluates certain standards of performance. These performance indicators need to be measured daily, weekly, and monthly, depending on their purpose.

11. Managing owners need to be passionate about their roles as managing owner. They must want to do the job, and at the same time, the firm must want them to be the managing owner.

12. The managing owner needs to be focused on developing the next managing owner. The goal should be to develop someone who can do the job better than the existing person. Firms that do not accomplish the proper transition between managing owners will not be competitive in the future, and many will not survive the next generation.

13. Finally, the managing owner needs to be able to make tough decisions in a thoughtful, decisive manner. Any decision must be in the best interests of the firm and can never, not ever, be made based on how it affects the managing owner. The level of integrity on personal benefits to the managing owner must be beyond reproach.[1]

Example Two—David Morgan

David Morgan, the co-managing owner of Lattimore Black Morgan & Cain, P.C., the largest locally owned CPA firm in Tennessee, had this to say:

The role of managing partner (MP) cannot simply be to warm a seat in the corner office resting in an "ivory tower" of personal accomplishments. It is critical to the success of an organization that the MP's role be one of leading with values, providing vision for the future, and involvement with personnel and clients.

LEAD WITH VALUES

In Lattimore Black Morgan & Cain, we display our core purpose and our core values in prominent places throughout our offices. However, as MP it is my responsibility to make sure we really believe and live by our core values. Ours include:

- **R**espect and concern for our clients and for each other
- **E**xtraordinary competence
- **A**bsolute integrity
- **C**ontinuous innovation and learning
- **H**igh expectations and accountability, and
- **C**ommitment to a balanced quality of life

---

[1]Steve Mayer, "What Do Managing Partners Do?" *Partner Advantage Advisory* 2, no. 6 (2004): 7. Reprinted with permission.

MPs must set the example for others to follow. If we do not adhere to our core values, how can we ever establish a culture in which all employees are expected to follow these values? Occasionally, we may find an employee that does not embrace the values of the organization or is unable to meet our high expectations. In these situations, to preserve the culture of the firm, it is often necessary that the person leave our organization. These are tough decisions, but when handled properly, demonstrate a respect for all involved and a genuine concern for the overall organization as well as for the departing individual. It is the MP's responsibility to ensure that such actions are carried out amicably and professionally.

Absolute integrity must be consistently demonstrated by the MP. The old saying "do what I say, not what I do" does not apply here. People mirror what we demonstrate and there is no substitute for anything less than absolute integrity. If the firm is to truly embrace the core values which form the firm's culture, this must be a top-down approach beginning with the MP. Our firm has an ongoing process by which we survey both clients and staff to support and strengthen our core values. The utilization of an independent survey provides us with honest and unbiased feedback from our clients and employees. Based on this information, when we see areas that need improvement, we immediately address the issue and work to make it "right." Unchanging core values can co-exist within an ever-changing environment. Our values provide the framework necessary to embrace the constant change that is necessary for success.

STRATEGY AND GROWTH

The MP must always be thinking ahead. No successful business can remain static; it is either moving forward or backward. While the MP often gets involved in the day-to-day tactics of executing strategy, we must also be thinking strategically and spending the time necessary to evaluate the best place to allocate scarce resources of time and money. Many firms simply live for today, enjoying their success to the fullest by draining the firm through current compensation for the owners. Firms like these can be very successful in the short run, but are doomed in the long run as this approach provides little opportunity for growth. We must allocate resources for the young "stars" in our organization because they represent our future. Positioning the firm for the future requires a strong commitment to investing in technology, new people, and new services that will provide for future growth and firm success.

If you embrace the concept that growth is necessary to retain the best people by providing them opportunities for outstanding careers, the MP should be involved in all major business development opportunities. This involvement demonstrates to prospective clients they are important to the firm and there will be a commitment of resources to ensure they are served well. This involvement by the MP also demonstrates to the entire firm the importance of developing new business.

THE VOICE

The MP is the firm's public voice. Whether it is telling the firm's story in a short and concise manner at a mixer with attorneys or communicating the firm's vision for the future to all employees at an annual "State of the Firm" meeting, the MP must be a good communicator. When approached by the media, he or she must use good judgment in what is communicated, understanding that sometimes it is best to remain silent. It is always important to remember the MP represents a large group of clients and other key stakeholders that often have differing or competing objectives and it is important to honor each of them.

TALENT SEARCH

The current upheaval in our profession is providing great growth opportunities for the well positioned firm. To take advantage of these opportunities, the MP must help attract top level talent to the firm. Entry level personnel recruitment can be delegated to others, but many firms are beginning to involve the MP in the latter stages of recruitment. When it comes to experienced talent, however, the MP *must* be involved. For recruits who have the potential to significantly impact a specific practice area, the MP must communicate the vision of the firm so they clearly see opportunity and how they could fit into that vision. This is especially important as personnel are recruited to spearhead new practice areas.

PROBLEM SOLVING

While many of the MP's duties can be stimulating and fun, some are not. One of the greatest challenges comes when MPs must function as the "Complaint Department." Problems need to be addressed quickly and effectively to prevent them from growing into larger issues. Unfortunately, many professionals tend to avoid conflict resolution, hoping the problem will just go away. MPs must maintain an open door and be ready to assist in resolving employee and client issues alike. They must also maintain open eyes and ears to recognize small problems before they become larger ones. This is not to suggest that responsibility should not be delegated so employee issues are handled by immediate supervisors whenever possible. However, when problems escalate, MPs must step in and assist in resolution. The same approach applies to client problems. MPs must assume the role of counselor, mediator, facilitator, and peacemaker. Often when a client is unhappy, professional egos can come into play and rather than "fixing the problem," some individuals try to "affix the blame." The MP must bring an objective viewpoint and remove emotion from situations to prevent them from escalating into more severe issues.

Finally, MPs must remind themselves and owners that success is never final. They must create a culture that embraces change, including the change that will one day occur when a new MP takes over.[2]

Example Three—Tom Feeley

Tom Feeley, the managing owner of Feeley & Driscoll, P.C. in Boston, provided us with eight tasks that rank high on his list.

---

[2]David K. Morgan, CPA, "What Managing Partners Do: Committed to Leading the Way," *Partner Advantage Advisory* 2, no. 9 (2004): 1, 6. Reprinted with permission.

1. Feeley says, "Managing owners should monitor and create reports on client profitability. Each client is rated, A, B, C and D. The A clients made more money than ever; B clients made good money; C clients had small losses but are in control; and D clients are out of control. Most of the clients that come into Feeley & Driscoll are C or D type clients. Feeley is successful because we make these clients A or B type clients." How many of your clients have you brought to the A or B level?

2. Managing owners need to enforce CPE. Feeley says, "Forget the 40-hour-a-year rule. Make your owners and staff spend more than 100 hours a year developing new skills and competencies." How many hours per year do your owners spend developing new skills?

3. According to Feeley, "Managing owners need to make sure their owners and staff take annual vacations. In today's high-pressure environment, our people need to have a healthy balance between work and life. Vacations are critical for the high level of client service that is needed throughout the year." How can you help revitalize your people? Do all your owners take annual vacations?

4. Managing owners should spend time counseling and coaching owners and fast-track people. How much time do you spend doing this during the year?

5. Managing owners should constantly be talking about the firm's strategic vision and its competitive advantage. Feeley encourages all managing owners to remember the old MBWA (managing by walking around) technique. How many hours per week do you spend walking the halls in your firm?

6. Managing owners need to teach the art of collaborating. For whatever reason, accountants are not good collaborators. "They don't get others involved with 'their' clients," according to Feeley. Collaborators learn from others. They do not let their egos get in the way. They are not afraid to bring other professionals into contact with their clients. How good are you at collaborating?

7. Managing owners need to get the message out to all staff members. They need to be seen often and communicate regularly. How much time do you spend with staff members during the course of a month?

8. Managing owners worry about the firm's culture. They strive to nurture it into what it is supposed to be. They often ensure the firm is performing upward evaluations and skip-level interviews (interviews in which people are not giving feedback to their immediate supervisors, but rather their supervisor's supervisor). What do you do to ensure that everyone is living your firm's values?"[3]

If your managing owner is not doing these eight things, perhaps he or she is merely an administrative owner.

---

[3]"What do managing partners do" Q & Answers, *Partner Advantage Advisory* 2, no. 10 (2004): 8. Answered by Tom Feeley. Reprinted with permission.

WHAT IS AN ADMINISTRATIVE OWNER?

While the administrative owner often maintains the title of managing owner, he or she is generally not involved in the activities we previously described. Rather, administrative owners handle the firm's administrative responsibilities (for example, budgets, facilities, reports and record keeping, human resources issues, technology, and so on). They operate like managers, who concentrate on tasks and activities and ensure things *get* done, rather than like leaders, who focus on vision and strategy and clarify what *needs* to be done.

WHAT IS A REAL MANAGING OWNER WORTH?

In the corporate world the CEO is usually the highest paid individual in the company. According to Carl A. Leonard, a consultant at Hildebrandt International, it is not a coincidence that the highest paid person in a business entity is almost always the chief executive. Why? This person has the most influence over the success or failure of the business. He suggests that owners in law firms (and we agree that owners in accounting firms) seem to accept this proposition for their business clients, but often fail to see why it should apply to their businesses.

Owners in many CPA firms do not recognize the leadership value a good managing owner can bring to the firm. While none of the three managing owners we quoted above mentioned profits, you can be sure these firms are highly profitable. Effective leadership provides the firm with a competitive advantage and, above all, profits. In many firms, owners often want to evaluate their managing owners based on the number of billable hours or new business they generate. Leadership is often not high on the list.

WHAT ARE MANAGING OWNERS PAID?

The answer to this question depends, in part, on whether the managing owner operates at the executive or administrative level. In most firms with which we have worked, the executive level managing owner is the highest paid owner. When this is not the case, they usually still remain in the top quartile even when the managing owner has little or no book of business. Under new compensation systems the managing owner is often compensated with a base plus a bonus tied to achieving overall firm goals. The bonus can be 100 percent or more of the base salary. In other firms, the managing owner receives a base plus a specific dollar amount (in the form of a stipend) for taking on the managing owner role as well as a bonus.

FINAL THOUGHTS

A strong managing owner with vision, drive, charisma, courage, and strong leadership skills often helps a firm achieve significant long-term results. Without a strong managing owner, firms often struggle—emotionally, operationally, and financially. Coral's grandmother, while never having been a managing partner, had the common sense to know the secret of being successful in the position (or any other). Here is one of her favorite sayings that would aptly apply to the role of managing owner today, "Honey, no one notices when there's no dust on the furniture. They only notice when there is." Similarly, a managing owner is invisible when things go well and very visible when they do not.

14

WHAT WILL YOU DO TOMORROW?

"When it comes to the future, there are three kinds of people:
those who let it happen, those who make it happen,
and those who wonder what happened."

—Ron M. Richardson, Jr.

Congratulations for finishing the book. By now we trust you have a more in-depth understanding of differing types of compensation plans. And we hope the majority of your questions about these plans are answered. Our goal was to provide you with information that allows you to improve or recreate your compensation system. It is now time for you to choose whether you will do either. As the above quote states, you have only three options, do nothing, do something, or wonder.

If you are thinking about implementing a new plan, you may still be unsure about which owner and staff compensation plan is right for your firm. When it comes to compensation, there are almost as many formulas for splitting the pie as there are firms. Our 2006 Compensation Survey surely demonstrates this. Nevertheless, we want to leave you with some concrete steps to follow and some recommendations. For it is up to you to decide.

FOUR KEYS TO SUCCESS

There is a fairly simple four-step process to follow when improving or recreating your owner and employee compensation systems.

1. Diagnose before you prescribe. When you visit your doctor with symptoms, he or she must diagnose before prescribing medication or treatment. Be sure you know the underlying problems—not just the symptoms—of your current plan. To assist you in this step see Exhibit 14–1, "Diagnostic Questionnaire."
2. Involve everyone in the diagnosis and design—get their input. Involvement is absolutely essential for a successful program. We often say, "no involvement, no commitment." This does not mean, however, you must gain consensus. The ultimate decision rests with the firm's management team.

3. Understand that individual behavior drives firm-wide culture. Each firm will design its own compensation program, and it should motivate individuals to live the firm's values, develop their competencies, and hit their performance goals, thus creating desired culture. Your compensation plan will not change the firm's culture, so make sure you start with developing the culture you want and then design the compensation plan to support that culture.

4. Be sure *everyone* understands the new plan—and owners buy into it. You cannot spend too much time educating staff members and owners about their programs. They must understand how it will work, how it will be funded and who will administer it.

CONSIDERATIONS

Whenever you try something new, you can almost be sure it will not be perfect the first time. The same is true for compensation programs. To come as close as possible to perfection, however, here are things you need to consider:

- *What factors will be part of your new plan?* Determine what factors you will measure and how you will measure them. The factors on which people will be measured should motivate them to behave in a manner that furthers the firm's strategic initiatives.

- *What weight will you assign for each factor?* Depending on your strategic initiatives, the factors on which you measure should have different weights, and the weights can and should change from year to year based on changes in your strategic initiatives.

- *What tool(s) will you use to measure each factor?* You can use 360-degree surveys, productivity reports from the time and billing system, marketing reports, satisfaction surveys, and a wide variety of other tools to measure the factors.

- *Does the compensation system recognize all types of contribution to the firm's success?* Firms need strong finders, minders, and grinders as well as leaders, mentors, coaches, and so on, to be successful. Firms are a composite of the knowledge, skills, and personal attributes of its owners and employees. Fortunately, people are not clones of one another, and your compensation system needs to recognize the various contributions that drive the firm's overall success. While it is true that not everyone is created equal, it is also true that the firm would not be where it is today without everyone contributing, in some fashion, to its success.

- *Is it perceived to be fair?* A system that is not perceived to be fair or fairly applied is doomed to cause problems. We suggest, therefore, that you seek feedback at least annually to determine existing beliefs about the compensation systems' fairness.

- *Is it flexible to meet changing needs of the firm?* Firms definitely change and you want to ensure the program is flexible enough to change along with the firm. We are not suggesting frequent changes in the compensation system, however. We suggest changes only to the degree they are absolutely necessary.

■ *Does it have significant differentials in compensation from owner to owner (or team member to team member)?* Small variances in total compensation (that is, salary plus bonus) between people in the same role (especially senior roles) are not healthy. As we said, owners and employees are neither clones nor equal contributors. The longer your system is in place, the greater the gap in compensation between the highest performer and the lowest performer in each level at the firm.

BENEFITS

While we like to say all firms should embrace a pay for performance system, we know that is not going to happen. Nevertheless, there are benefits that only a pay for performance system can bring. Pay for performance:

1. Provides a clear link to the firm's strategic plan, and core values.
2. Is transparent.
3. Links individual and team performance to pay.
4. Provides fair, honest, and accurate assessments of performance.
5. Rewards high performers and identifies low performers.
6. Ties into competencies which reflect the skills and abilities needed to meet firm goals.

FINAL THOUGHTS

Donald Trump once said, "In the end, you're measured not by how much you undertake, but by what you finally accomplish." Designing the right compensation plan is a great undertaking to help you and your firm accomplish desired results.

The choice is now yours. Choose wisely.

EXHIBIT 14–1   **Diagnostic Questionnaire**

1. What is your current compensation system (formula, equity, equal pay, executive committee or managing owner decides, pay-for-performance)?

2. What do your owners like about it?

3. What do your owners dislike about it?

4. Do they perceive it to be fair?

5. Do they understand how the compensation process works?

6. What factors are currently measured?

7. Do these factors drive the desired behavior?

8. Do the owners fill out a self-evaluation form at the end of the year?

9. Is the self-evaluation form shared with the other owners?

10. Is input sought from all the other owners regarding compensation decisions?

11. Do you provide owners with a base salary and then allocate profits based on specific criteria?

12. What percentage of an owner's compensation is the base salary?

13. What percentage of total compensation comes from the bonus pool?

14. Does the plan drive the desired results?

2006 OWNER COMPENSATION SURVEY

Conducted by
August J. Aquila, Ph.D. and Coral L. Rice
Sponsored by
PCPS Division of the AICPA

2006 Owner Compensation Survey
Overall Results

What type of owner compensation system does the firm currently use?	N	%
Equal pay method	67	15.8
Formula method (firm uses algebraic formula to determine income allocation)	75	17.7
Managing owner decides how to allocate income	53	12.5
Compensation committee (small group of owners) decides how to allocate income	22	5.2
Executive committee decides how to allocate income	21	5.0
All owners (meet as a group) to decide how to allocate income	47	11.1
Pay-for-Performance method (objective and subjective goals are predetermined for each owner at the beginning of the year and evaluated at the end of the year)4	23	5.
Paper and Pencil method (all owners recommend a base compensation for each owner including themselves)	10	2.4
Ownership percentage method (income allocate based on ownership percentage)	28	6.6
Eat what you kill (system only rewards individual production effort)	23	5.4
Other (please specify)	55	13.0
Total Respondents	424	

For how many years have you been using this method?	*N*	*%*
1 year or less	13	3.1
2 to 5 years	81	19.6
5 or more years	320	77.3
Total Respondents	414	

Compared to 10 years ago, how much has your compensation system changed?	*N*	*%*
Hasn't changed	185	45.2
Somewhat changed	142	34.7
Significantly changed	82	20.0
Total Respondents	409	

How likely is it that your firm will change its owner compensation system in the next two years?	*N*	*%*
Not likely	211	51.1
Somewhat likely	124	30.0
Very likely	64	15.5
Not sure	14	3.4
Total Respondents	413	

How satisfied are you with the current system?	*N*	*%*
Very dissatisfied	20	4.9
Somewhat dissatisfied	41	10.1
Neither satisfied nor dissatisfied	31	7.6
Somewhat satisfied	181	44.5
Very satisfied	134	32.9
Total Respondents	407	

How satisfied do you believe your fellow owners are with the current system?	*N*	*%*
Very dissatisfied	14	3.4
Somewhat dissatisfied	44	10.8
Neither satisfied nor dissatisfied	42	10.3
Somewhat satisfied	194	47.7
Very satisfied	95	23.3
Total Respondents	407	

If you were to select a new compensation system, which one would you select from the following?	N	%
Equal pay method	13	3.4
Formula method (firm uses algebraic formula to determine income allocation)	71	18.3
Managing owner decides how to allocate income	18	4.6
Compensation committee (small group of owners) decides how to allocate income	29	7.5
Executive committee decides how to allocate income	18	4.6
All owners (meet as a group) to decide how to allocate income	37	9.5
Pay-for-Performance method (objective and subjective goals are predetermined for each owner at the beginning of the year and evaluated at the end of the year)	140	36.1
Paper and Pencil method (all owners recommend a base compensation for each owner including themselves)	7	1.8
Ownership percentage method (income allocate based on ownership percentage)	14	3.6
Eat what you kill (system only rewards individual production effort)	17	4.4
Other (please specify)	24	6.2
Total Respondents	388	

Below is a list of compensation criteria that you may or may not use in your current system. Please indicate if each particular factor is used or not used in your current system. If it is used, please indicate how important the factor is to your current system.	Currently used	Not currently used
Book of business	43% (155)	35% (126)
Client or book gross profitability (cash collected less total time at cost to service client or book)	23% (80)	58% (198)
Community involvement	19% (65)	63% (214)
Cross-selling	15% (52)	68% (230)
Fees collected	37% (129)	40% (141)
Firm management responsibility	43% (150)	33% (115)
Industry experience/expertise	13% (45)	65% (218)
Managed charge hours	30% (102)	48% (164)
Mentoring and training employees	20% (68)	60% (206)
New business development (origination)	35% (124)	40% (141)
Ownership percentage	40% (141)	35% (124)
Personal billable hours (all hours that were actually billed to client)	36% (126)	39% (136)
Personal charge hours (all hours that were charged to work-in-process)	32% (113)	45% (159)
Professional involvement	17% (57)	60% (205)

(continued)

Below is a list of compensation criteria that you may or may not use in your current system. Please indicate if each particular factor is used or not used in your current system. If it is used, please indicate how important the factor is to your current system.	*Currently used*	*Not currently used*
Realization (net fees divided by gross fees)	33% (115)	44% (153)
Seniority within the firm	21% (72)	56% (192)
Technical expertise	19% (65)	58% (195)
Utilization (total charge hours divided by total work hours)	13% (44)	65% (215)
Total Respondents	367	

Below is a list of compensation criteria that you may or may not use in your current system. Please indicate if each particular factor is used or not used in your current system. If it is used please indicate how important the factor is to your current system.	*Very unimportant*	*Somewhat unimportant*	*Somewhat important*	*Very important*
Book of business	4% (13)	5% (17)	24% (85)	26% (94)
Client or book gross profitability (cash collected less total time at cost to service client or book)	2% (8)	4% (15)	21% (73)	15% (50)
Community involvement	4% (15)	15% (52)	20% (67)	2% (6)
Cross-selling	4% (14)	9% (29)	19% (66)	3% (11)
Fees collected	4% (14)	5% (16)	24% (83)	25% (89)
Firm management responsibility	3% (12)	9% (32)	39% (139)	13% (46)
Industry experience/expertise	3% (9)	7% (24)	26% (87)	6% (19)
Managed charge hours	3% (12)	8% (26)	28% (97)	13% (45)
Mentoring and training employees	2% (7)	11% (39)	24% (82)	7% (23)
New business development (origination)	1% (5)	7% (23)	28% (98)	23% (82)
Ownership percentage	9% (32)	12% (41)	23% (81)	17% (61)
Personal billable hours (all hours that were actually billed to client)	3% (10)	7% (25)	31% (108)	18% (63)
Personal charge hours (all hours that were charged to work-in-process)	5% (17)	10% (35)	26% (91)	13% (47)
Professional involvement	4% (15)	15% (51)	20% (67)	4% (13)
Realization (net fees divided by gross fees)	3% (10)	8% (29)	28% (98)	16% (56)
Seniority within the firm	8% (26)	13% (43)	20% (68)	6% (19)
Technical expertise	3% (9)	8% (27)	26% (88)	10% (33)
Utilization (total charge hours divided by total work hours)	5% (17)	11% (36)	19% (62)	5% (18)
Total Respondents	367			

How satisfied are you with the current criteria?	*N*	*%*
Very dissatisfied	15	4.1
Somewhat dissatisfied	44	11.9
Neither satisfied nor dissatisfied	37	10.0
Somewhat satisfied	164	44.4
Very satisfied	108	29.3
Total Respondents	369	

How satisfied do you believe your fellow owners are with the current criteria?	*N*	*%*
Very dissatisfied	8	2.2
Somewhat dissatisfied	41	11.1
Neither satisfied nor dissatisfied	48	13.0
Somewhat satisfied	181	49.1
Very satisfied	83	22.5
Total Respondents	369	

Which of the following criteria do you believe should be used in your owner compensation system? (check all that apply)	*N*	*%*
Book of business	224	63.1
Client or book gross profitability (cash collected less total time at cost to service client or book)	214	60.3
Community involvement	147	41.4
Cross-selling	147	41.4
Fees collected	234	65.9
Firm management responsibility	294	82.8
Industry experience/expertise	129	36.3
Managed charge hours	183	51.5
Mentoring and training employees	192	54.1
New business development (origination)	261	73.5
Ownership percentage	168	47.3
Personal billable hours (all hours that were actually billed to client)	200	56.3
Personal charge hours (all hours that were charged to work-in-process)	137	38.6
Professional involvement	131	36.9
Realization (net fees divided by gross fees)	216	60.8
Seniority within the firm	95	26.8
Technical expertise	175	49.3
Utilization (total charge hours divided by total work hours)	99	27.9
Other (please specify)	22	6.2
Total Respondents	355	

How would you describe the way in which owner performance is currently evaluated?	*N*	*%*
Formal, written annual evaluation of performance	34	9.3
Informal, verbal (little written) evaluation of performance	140	38.4
Combination of formal and informal	62	17.0
There is currently no evaluation of owner performance	129	35.3
Total Respondents	365	

Evaluation is mainly:	*N*	*%*
Objective	45	14.7
Subjective	95	31.0
Combination of objective and subjective	166	54.2
Total Respondents	306	

To what extent . . .	*Not at all*	*To some extent*	*To a great extent*
Do you understand your firm's compensation system?	1% (2)	7% (24)	93% (337)
Does each owner understand your firm's compensation system?	1% (3)	24% (86)	75% (272)
Do you believe your firm's owner compensation system drives performance?	15% (56)	53% (191)	32% (115)
Total Respondents	363		

Please indicate the extent to which you believe the current owner compensation system is designed to be fair to each owner in the firm.	*N*	*%*
System is not designed to be fair.	31	8.5
System is designed to be somewhat fair.	145	39.8
System is designed to be very fair.	188	51.6
Total Respondents	364	

Please indicate the extent to which you believe the current owner compensation system is applied fairly to each owner in the firm.	*N*	*%*
System is not applied fairly.	20	5.5
System is applied somewhat fairly.	126	34.6
System is applied very fairly.	218	59.9
Total Respondents	364	

To what extent do you believe setting individual owner goals contributes to higher levels of firm profitability?

	N	%
Not at all	26	7.2
To some extent	194	54.0
To a great extent	139	38.7
Total Respondents	359	

Do you believe team/firm-wide goals tied to owner compensation are a useful process for achieving higher levels of profitability in the firm?

	N	%
Yes	306	85.2
No	53	14.8
Total Respondents	359	

Does each owner in your firm have written goals?

	N	%
Yes	71	19.6
No	291	80.4
Total Respondents	362	

Do you believe each owner should have written goals?

	N	%
Yes	292	80.9
No	69	19.1
Total Respondents	361	

To what extent is your owner compensation system tied into achieving results of your strategic plan?

	N	%
Not at all	190	52.9
To some extent	135	37.6
To a great extent	34	9.5
Total Respondents	359	

How much would you like the firm's revenue (top line) to increase over the next 5 years?

	N	%
1–5%	12	3.3
6–10%	64	17.8
11–15%	73	20.3
16%+	211	58.6
Total Respondents	360	

How much would you like the firm's profits to increase over the next 5 years?	*N*	*%*
1–5%	8	2.2
6–10%	54	15.0
11–15%	78	21.7
16%+	220	61.1
Total Respondents	360	

BIBLIOGRAPHY

Andersen, Michael. Partner Compensation Systems in Professional Services Firms, Part I. http://www.edge.ai/Edge-International-1057905.html; accessed on January 25, 2007.

_____. Partner Compensation systems in Professional Services Firms, Part II. http://www.edge.ai/Edge-International-1057907.html; accessed on January 25, 2007.

Aquila, August J., and Marcus, Bruce W. *Client at the Core: Marketing and Managing Today's Professional Services Firm.* Hoboken, N.J.: John Wiley & Sons, 2004.

Aquila, August J. "The Marketing Plan: An Audit-Based Approach," *The Marketing Advantage: How to Get and Keep the Clients You Want.* New York: AICPA, 1994.

_____. "Splitting the Pie." *Partner to Partner Advisory* (April 1999): 5.

_____. "New Thoughts on Partner Compensation." *Accounting Today* (June 5-18, 2006).

Ansoff, H. Igor. "Strategies for Diversification." *Harvard Business Review* (September/October 1957), pp. 113-124.

Baker, Ronald, and Dunn, Paul. *The Firm of the Future.* Hoboken, N.J.: John Wiley & Sons, 2003.

Barker, Joel Arthur. *Paradigms: The Business of Discovering the Future.* New York: Harper Business, 1993.

Brotherton, Phaedra, and Hayes, Michael. "Meyners Mines Its Talent." *Journal of Accountancy* (September 2002), pp. 47-50.

Brotherton, Phaedra. "Meyners Pays for Performance." *Journal of Accountancy* (July 2003), p. 41.

Buckingham, Marcus, and Curt Coffman. *First, Break All the Rules: What the World's Greatest Managers Do Differently.* New York: Simon & Schuster, 1999.

Chingos, Peter T. *Paying for Performance: A Guide to Compensation Management.* 2d ed. Hoboken, N.J.: John Wiley and Sons, 2002.

Collins, Jim. *Good to Great: Why Some Companies Make The Leap . . . and Others Don't.* New York: Harper Collins Publishers, Inc., 2001.

Cotterman, James D. "Making Better Compensation Decisions," Report to Legal Management, Altman Weil Inc., April 2006.

Covey, Stephen R. *Principle Centered Leadership.* New York: Fireside Press, 1992.

_____. *The 7 Habits of Highly Effective People.* New York: Fireside Press, 1989.

_____. *The 8th Habit: From Effectiveness to Greatness.* New York: Free Press, 2004

Drucker, Peter. *The Drucker Foundation Self-Assessment Tool (Participant Workbook).* San Francisco: Jossey-Bass, 1999.

Fajt, Marissa. "Firms Focus on College Grads to Fill Accountant Shortage." *Austin Business Journal* (March 17, 2006).

Feeley, Tom. "What Do Managing Partners Do?" *Partner Advantage Advisory 2*, no. 10 (2004): 8.

Hamel, Gary, and C. K. Prahalad. *Competing for the Future.* Boston: Harvard Business School, 1994.

Hayes, Michael. "Pay for Performance." *Journal of Accountancy* (June 2002).

Hays, Scott. "Pros and Cons of Pay for Performance." *Workforce Online* (February 1999).

Heskett, James L., Jones, Thomas O., Loveman, Gary W., Sasser, W. Earl, and Schlesinger, Leonard A. "Putting the Service-Profit Chain to Work." *Harvard Business Review* (March-April 1994).

Heskett, James L., Sasser, W. Earl Jr., and Schlesinger, Leonard A. *The Service Profit Chain.* New York: The Free Press, 1997.

Jorgensen, Karen. *Pay for Results: A Practical Guide to Effective Employee Compensation.* Santa Monica, Calif.: Merritt Publishing, 1966.

Kaplan, Herbert M. "Marketing Fundamentals: Terms and Concepts," *The Marketing Advantage: How to Get and Keep the Clients You Want.* New York: AICPA, 1994.

Kaplan, Robert S. and Norton, David P. *Translating Strategy into Action: The Balanced Scorecard.* Boston: Harvard Business School Press, 1996.

_____. *Strategy Maps: Converting Intangible Assets into Tangible Outcome.* Boston: Harvard Business School Press, 2004.

Kohn, Alfie. *Punished by Rewards: The Trouble with Gold Stars, Incentive Plans, A's, Praise, and other Bribes.* New York: Houghton Mifflin Co., 1999.

Lagace, Martha. "Pay-for-Performance Doesn't Always Pay Off," *HBS Working Knowledge*, April 14, 2003.

Lencioni, Patrick. *Overcoming the FIVE Dysfunctions of a TEAM: a Leadership Fable.* San Francisco: Jossey-Bass. 2005.

MacKay, Karen. "Selecting the Compensation Committee: The Power of Balancing Personalities," Edge International Review. Winter 2005.

Maister, David. *Practice What You Preach.* New York: The Free Press, Simon & Schuster, 2001.

_____. "Stop Paying for Performance" *Passion, People and Principles*—www.davidmaister.com/blog, April 2006.

Marcus, Bruce W. *Competing for Clients.* Chicago: Probus Publishing Company, 1981.

_____. *Competing for Clients in the 90s: A Dynamic Guide to Marketing, Promoting & Building a Professional Services Practice.* Chicago: Probus Publishing Company, 1992.

_____. *The Marcus Letter on Professional Services Marketing.* www.marcusletter.com.

Mastracchio, Nicholas J., Jr. *Mergers and Acquisitions of CPA Firms: A Guide to Practice Valuation.* New York: American Institute of Certified Public Accountants, 1998.

Mayer, Steve. "What Do Managing Partners Do?" *Partner Advantage Advisory* 2, no. 6 (2004): 7.

Morgan, David K. "What Managing Partners Do: Committed to Leading the Way," *Partner Advantage Advisory* 2, no. 9 (2004): 1, 6.

Niven, Paul R. *Balanced Scorecard Step-by-Step: Maximizing Performance and Maintaining Results*, New Jersey: John Wiley & Son, 2002.

Pfeffer, Jeffrey. "Six Dangerous Myths about Pay." *Harvard Business Review* (May-June 1998): 109-119.

Prescott, Blane R. "Follow the Money—The Evolution of Partner Compensation Systems in Law Firms" (December 21, 1999), Hildebrandt International http://www.hildebrandt.com/Documents.aspx?Doc_ID=912.

Rice, Coral L. "What's More Important: What People Undertake or What People Accomplish," *AICPA PCPS Firm Practice Center*, 2005.

Rose, Joel A, "Newer trends in determining the most appropriate partner compensation system for your firm and standards to assess partner performance." (http://www.joelarose.com/articles/newer_trends_partner_compensation.html.

Rosenberg, Marc L. "Not All Partners Are Created Equal: Essential Elements of an Effective Partner Compensation System." *Insight* (May 1977): 9.

Ruiz, Gina, "Lessons From the Front Lines." *Workforce Management* (June 26, 2006): 50-52.

Shechtman, Morri, "Five Steps to Becoming a Stronger Leader: A Challenge for 2004." *Partner Advantage Advisory*, 2004.

Schuster, Jay R., and Zingheim, Patricia K. *The New Pay: Linking Employee and Organizational Performance.* San Francisco, Jossey-Bass Publishers, 1992.

Sewell, Carl. *Customers for Life: How to Turn that One-Time Buyer into Customers for Life.* New York, Currency by Doubleday, 1990.

Stern, Gary. *The Drucker Foundation Self-Assessment Tool (Process Guide).* San Francisco: Jossey-Bass, 1999.

Stimpson, Jeff, "The New Compensation Models." *Practical Accountant* (December 6, 2004).

Sujansky, Joanne G. "The Seven Mistakes Leaders Make." *Partner Advantage Advisory*, March 2004.

Telberg, Rick. "Boomers, X-ers and Y's: CPA Generation Gap is Real," www.CPA2Biz.com, February 2005.

"The Flaster/Greenberg Difference," http://www.flastergreenberg.com/careers/flasterdifference.cfm; 2006, Flaster/Greenberg.

Waterman, Robert, Peters, Thomas, and Phillips, Julien. "Structure is Not Organization." *Business Horizons*, June 1980, Volume 23, Issues 3. pp. 14-26.

Printed in the United States
By Bookmasters